Student Course Guide
for

Diane Martin, Ph.D.
Professor of English
Dallas County Community College District

Dallas TeleLearning
R. Jan LeCroy Center for Educational Telecommunications
Dallas County Community College District

For use with the second edition of *The Composition of Everyday Life: A Guide to Writing*
by John Mauk and John Metz

Australia • Brazil • Canada • Mexico • Singapore • Spain • United Kingdom • United States

The Design and Production Team

Content Specialist:	Diane Martin, Ph.D.
Instructional Designer:	Janice Christophel
Director of Production:	Craig Mayes
Producer/Director:	Julia Dyer
Production Coordinator:	Ruby Barrón
Telecommunications Information Specialist:	Evelyn J. Wong

R. Jan LeCroy Center for Educational Telecommunications

President:	Pamela K. Quinn
Vice-President, Distance Education:	James P. Picquet, Ph.D.
Dean of Financial Affairs:	Dorothy J. Clark
Dean of Distance Learning:	Edward C. Bowen
Dean, Marketing and Community Relations:	Rachelle Howell
Director of Product Development:	Bob Crook

NATIONAL ADVISORY COMMITTEE

Kathleen Dawson	Los Angeles Mission College
Michael Haddock	Florida Community College at Jacksonville
Valerie Hockert	Thomas Edison State College
Kim Jameson	Oklahoma City Community College
Jeffrey Miranda	Tarrant County Community College
Robyn Lyons-Robinson	Columbus State Community College

DCCCD ADVISORY COMMITTEE

Paul Benson	Mountain View College
Luisa Benton Forrest	El Centro College
Phyllis Elmore	North Lake College
Ed Garcia	Brookhaven College
Michael Morris	Eastfield College
Jane Peterson	Richland College
Rebekah Rios-Harris	Cedar Valley College

Student Course Guide ISBN (10): 1-4130-3396-2; ISBN (13): 978-1-4130-3396-0
Copyright 2008 by Dallas County Community College District

All rights reserved. No part of this work may be reproduced, stored in a retrieval system, or transcribed, in any form or by any means—electronic, mechanical, photocopying, recording, or otherwise—without the prior written permission of Dallas County Community College District.

Requests for permission to make copies of any part of the work should be mailed to:
Dallas TeleLearning
9596 Walnut Street
Dallas, Texas 75243

This edition has been printed directly from camera-ready copy.

Printed in the United States of America
2007 2008 2009 5 4 3 2 1

Contents

To the Student v

Course Organization vii

Course Guidelines ix

Introduction to Lesson Videos xi

Lessons   Page

1. Exploring the Process 1
2. Explaining Relationships 11
3. Observing Details 19
4. Analyzing Concepts 27
5. Analyzing Images 37
6. Building Arguments 45
7. Responding to Arguments 51
8. Evaluating and Organizing 57
9. Integrating Research 69
10. Searching for Causes 81
11. Imagining Solutions 87
12. Discovering Voice 93
13. Thinking Radically 101

To the Student

Welcome to *The Writer's Circle!* You are about to embark upon a writing adventure. Whether you are a lover of writing or not, this course will provide you with the necessary skills, motivation, and tools to understand the writing process and succeed in the college classroom. I encourage you to take advantage of all the tools provided in this engaging course.

The text for this course, *The Composition of Everyday Life* by John Mauk and John Metz, provides the backdrop and instructional information to complete the requirements of this course. When the development team began work, we talked with the authors to discover their philosophy of the writing process and to understand their approach to teaching composition. What you see here is the result of collaboration. I wish to extend my personal thank you to both John Mauk and John Metz for consulting with me as we went through the process of developing this course.

The video series, *The Writer's Circle,* provides you the opportunity to learn more about the course content and to experience distance-learning students working in collaboration to prepare their assignments. The program hosts, or "gurus," will engage you in a light-hearted manner as they provide instructional content for the course. The five diverse students in our writer's group learn from each other as they exchange ideas, suggestions, and feedback about their assignments and their writing. Sometimes the students struggle with organization, or beginnings and endings; sometimes they find a clear writer's voice. Always the students in the videos are involved in the course and in their own writing process. I challenge you to become involved in this course and in your own writing. I challenge you to collaborate with others, whether it be your classmates, your spouse, your friends, or your children.

Pay particular attention in the course videos to the professional writers who address specific nuances of each lesson. What is voice? How do I create a good introduction? What organizational structure should I follow? How often should I revise? The writers come from many different areas of the writing world: poets, news editors, essayists, novelists, memoirists. Their experiences and expertise will encourage your writing. Also included in the course videos are "Quick Tips" – short, animated suggestions about very specific topics that can improve your writing, for example, transitional words and phrases.

This *Student Course Guide for The Writer's Circle* provides you with guidelines for each lesson. Each chapter outlines the lesson goal and objectives, assignments from the text (including a handbook), and enrichment activities that will assist you in delving deeper into the course. Remember the old saying, "Patience is a virtue." As you extend your patience, the text, the videos, the interactive activities, and the *Student Course Guide* all encourage you to dig deeper, think precisely, and pursue the wonders of the English language.

I have been an online and classroom instructor for over thirty-five years. Developing this course has been a capstone experience in my career. The gifts of my years of teaching are evident in this course. Please apply your capabilities as you explore the process and joy of writing. Broaden your horizons. Extend your thinking. Write…revise…and rewrite until you achieve your goal.

—Diane Martin

Course Organization

The Writer's Circle is designed as a comprehensive learning package consisting of four elements: student course guide, textbook, video programs, and interactive activities.

STUDENT COURSE GUIDE

The Student Course Guide for this course:

Martin, Diane. *Student Course Guide for The Writer's Circle.* Boston, MA: Thomson Wadsworth, 2008. ISBN (10): 1-413-03396-2; ISBN (13): 978-1-413-03396-0

This student course guide acts as your daily instructor. Each lesson gives you lesson resources, lesson goals, learning objectives, lesson focus points, suggested writing assignments, and enrichment activities. If you follow the student course guide recommendations, read the text assignment, and view each lesson carefully, you should successfully accomplish all of the requirements for this course.

TEXTBOOK

In addition to the student course guide, the textbook for this course is:

Mauk, John and John Metz. *The Composition of Everyday Life: A Guide to Writing.* 2nd ed. Boston, MA: Thomson Wadsworth, 2007. ISBN (10): 1-413-01849-1; ISBN (13): 978-1-413-01849-3

VIDEO PROGRAMS

The video program series for this course is:

The Writer's Circle

Each video program is correlated to a specific reading assignment for that lesson. The video programs are packed with information, so watch them closely.

If the lessons are broadcast more than once in your area, or if DVDs are available at your college, you might find it helpful to watch the video programs again for review. Since examination questions may be taken from the video programs as well as from the textbook, careful attention to both is vital to your success.

COMPUTER-BASED ACTIVITIES

Computer-graded interactive exercises and activities are available to students whose institutions have opted to offer these. These activities are useful for reinforcement and review of lesson content and learning objectives. The interactive activities are offered in two formats: CD-ROM and Internet. Ask your instructor how to access these activities if they are listed in your syllabus as a course requirement.

Course Guidelines

Follow these guidelines as you study the material presented in each lesson:

1. THEME—
   Read the Theme for an introduction to the lesson material.

2. LESSON RESOURCES—
   Review the Lesson Resources in order to schedule your time appropriately. Pay careful attention—the titles and numbers of the textbook chapters, the student course guide lessons, and the video programs may be different from one another.

3. LESSON GOAL—
   Review the Lesson Goal to learn what you are expected to know or be able to do upon completion of the lesson.

4. LESSON LEARNING OBJECTIVES—
   Review the Learning Objectives to guide you in successfully mastering the lesson content and achieving the Lesson Goal.

5. LESSON FOCUS POINTS—
   Pay attention to the Lesson Focus Points to get the most from your reading and viewing. You may want to write responses or notes to reinforce what you learn as you progress through the lesson material.

6. WRITERS INTERVIEWED—
   In Writers Interviewed, we gratefully acknowledge the expertise and assistance offered in the production of *The Writer's Circle* video programs by the individuals and institutions listed.

7. SUGGESTED WRITING ASSIGNMENTS—
   The Suggested Writing Assignments are offered as suggestions to help you apply the material presented in the lesson. Consult with your instructor and your course syllabus about the requirements for any of the assignments listed.

8. ENRICHMENT ACTIVITIES—
   The Enrichment Activities will help you evaluate your understanding of the material in this lesson. Use the Answer Key located at the end of the lesson to check your answers or reference material related to each question.

9. ANSWER KEY—
   The Answer Key provides answers and references for the Enrichment Activity questions.

Introduction to Lesson Videos

The video lessons of *The Writer's Circle* consist of two distinct but complementary elements: instructional segments that explain concepts and discuss writing tools and strategies, and narrative segments that model the writing process and focus attention on key aspects of the lesson. As you delve into *The Writer's Circle*, you will find that different segments help you accomplish lesson objectives in different ways.

Instructional segments are short, lively sessions hosted by two writing "Gurus," who explain and illustrate the main lesson components. Their teaching points are amplified by commentary from a variety of professional writers, who share their experience and wisdom on the topic at hand. Most lessons are also punctuated with "Quick Tips," animated shorts focusing on specific writing pointers and common pitfalls. This combination of targeted short subjects, interviews with writers, and direct instruction from the Gurus serves to introduce new material and deepen your understanding of the skills and strategies of good writing.

Interlaced with the instruction is an ongoing narrative storyline, in which a diverse group of students forms a writer's circle for their mutual support while taking an online composition course. They meet regularly in a neighborhood café to discuss assignments and share their work. In each program, you will follow one or more of the students as they undertake the actual writing assignment for that lesson: investigating a topic, refining a thesis, drafting an essay, getting feedback, and rewriting. As their stories unfold, you gain insight into the challenges, frustrations and rewards of producing a thoughtful, provocative piece of writing.

The main characters of *The Writer's Circle* are diverse in age and gender, and represent a broad range of social, racial and ethnic backgrounds. Individually they represent the wide variety of students who can benefit from improving their writing, while as a group they model the invaluable support a writer's group can give throughout the writing process. The writer's group includes:

- **Marcus:** Asian-American, early twenties, university student. Taking an on-line writing class on top of a full academic load. Majoring in political science and minoring in film studies.
- **Jada**: African-American, late twenties, Army Reserve. Served in combat in Iraq and is now going to college on the GI bill. Writes a personal blog called JadaSaysSo.
- **Lakshmi:** Indian immigrant, mid-thirties, single mother. Currently working, but wants to be a technical writer to improve her earning capacity.
- **Rosa:** Latino, mid-forties, paralegal. Married, children grown or in college. Nurses a secret ambition to go to law school.
- **Richard:** Anglo, early sixties, widowed. Retired early after starting and running a successful business. Now interested in creative pursuits, especially investigating and writing about his genealogy.

Lesson 1

Exploring the Process

In memory's telephoto lens, far objects are magnified.
—John Updike

THEME

For this first lesson, you will be asked to write about a memory from your past. "Why?" you might ask. In a first semester college writing course, thinking and writing about what you know is the best way to begin. Writing about a memory is self-reflective and involves looking back into what you know best, your individual history, to determine an event, a situation, or a set of events to remember in writing.

Determining what you will write about does not involve huge moments. More likely, you will recall small and seemingly unimportant moments that have taken on deeper meaning over a period of time. Images are the key to your remembering: check old photographs, visit a place from your past, do something you have not done for years, call or write someone from your past.

Once you find a topic, try to discover the significance of the past event. Maybe the event is significant because of the difference in perspectives between your past and the present. Why is the memory important for you, the writer? For your reader? Whatever your memory, the reader should feel a connection with the memory and be able to discover meaning in your experience. In establishing this connection, you will create what the text refers to as "public resonance." In other words, you will be addressing the writer and reader's shared relationship with an issue. This resonance is critical to achieving the lesson goal of discovering something meaningful about the past that can be shared with others and valued by them.

It's surprising how much of memory is built around things unnoticed at the time.
—Barbara Kingsolver

LESSON RESOURCES

Textbook: Mauk and Metz: *The Composition of Everyday Life*
- "Note to Students," pp. xxxv–xlii
- Chapter 1, "Remembering Who You Were," pp. 2–49
- Chapter 13, "Research and Writing"; "Punctuating Quotations," pp. 644–648
- Chapter 15, "Rhetorical Handbook"
  - "Punctuation," pp. 778–785
  - "How Sentences Work: A Look at Basic Grammar," pp. 786–789

Video: "Exploring the Process" from the series *The Writer's Circle*

LESSON GOAL

You will write a narrative that communicates an insight into a past experience by practicing the processes of invention, delivery, and revision.

LESSON LEARNING OBJECTIVES

1. Apply the writing process (invention, delivery, revision) to a narrative about the past.
2. Explore in depth a specific event or situation from the past.
3. Illustrate a particular insight about the event or situation from the past that led to a revelation or new perspective.
4. Apply strategies to create voice in a narrative about a specific event or situation from the past.
5. Revise the narrative of the past through a peer review process.

LESSON FOCUS POINTS

1. What is narration? How is narration useful to writers?
2. What are literary allusions?
3. How does a writer effectively use dialogue in narration?
4. How do details help writers when they remember a past event?
5. How does a writer begin when writing about a past event?
6. How does a writer conclude when writing about a past event?
7. What is writer's voice?
8. How does a writer's voice appear in choosing details?
9. How can literary allusions help create voice?
10. How can sentence length create voice?
11. What is figurative language? What is a metaphor? Simile? Understatement? Hyperbole?
12. How is peer review helpful in the revision of essays?

WRITERS INTERVIEWED

Jenny Anmuth, Travel Editor and Writer, Frommer's Travel Guides, South Salem, NY
Carol Berkin, Historian and Author, Baruch College, City University of New York, New York, NY
Eric Jerome Dickey, Novelist, Los Angeles, CA
Macarena Hernandez, Editorial Columnist, *The Dallas Morning News,* Dallas TX
Laeta Kalogridis, Screenwriter, Encino, CA
Naomi Shihab Nye, Author and Poet, San Antonio, TX
Richard Rodriguez, Essayist and Journalist, San Francisco, CA
Matt Zoller Seitz, Film and Television Critic, *New York Press/Newark Star Ledger,* Brooklyn, NY

SUGGESTED WRITING ASSIGNMENTS

Consult with your instructor and the course syllabus about requirements for any of the assignments listed below.

1. Write a narrative essay about a past event that includes appropriate details.
2. Rewrite a first draft of a "remembering" paper to turn in to your instructor along with your first draft. Clearly mark the revised draft for your instructor's response.
3. Ask as many of your friends, relatives, colleagues, classmates as possible to read your rewritten draft and to respond to it in writing using the guidelines in your text for peer review. Turn in at least three signed responses with the drafts you submit to your instructor.
4. Read the section in your text entitled, "Beyond the Essay" (p. 48). Respond in writing by considering an autobiography or biography you have read and how it made its point by presenting certain events or details in a person's life.
5. Read the section in your text entitled, "Beyond the Essay" (p. 48). Respond in writing by considering a biographical or autobiographical television show or movie you have seen. How did it make a particular point by the presentation of certain events or details in a person's life?
6. Aldous Huxley once said, "Every man's memory is his private literature." Respond to this quote according to your view of your own memory. What is your private literature? How much of it would you publish? How much would you keep private?

A memory is a beautiful thing; it's almost a desire that you miss.
—Gustave Flaubert

Lesson 1—Exploring the Process

ENRICHMENT ACTIVITIES

Complete the following activities. An answer key and/or guidelines appear at the end of this lesson for each activity.

I. Writing Activity: Creating Voice

Read the following passages taken from the essays written by the students in Lesson One of the course video. Identify the strategies each student used to create voice from the choices listed after each passage. Circle all that apply for each passage.

1. "There are concerts, there are great concerts, there are awesome concerts, and then there are concerts that are cataclysmic. They carry you away like a hurricane or a tornado; they flood your whole body. It's like a natural disaster without the disaster part, just pure audio power, leaving you senseless, delirious, and happily shattered."

   Marcus

   A. Simile
   B. Hyperbole
   C. Metaphor
   D. Sentence length

2. "There are some emotions that you just can't cook with. You can make a good curry when you're happy and you can make a good curry when you're angry, but you can't make a good curry when you're sad. I followed the recipe, but the curry came out all wrong. The spices drooped with sadness and the dish tasted like a bowl of curried tears."

   Lakshmi

   A. Simile
   B. Sentence length
   C. Metaphor
   D. Hyperbole

3. "No, I said, I'm going to be a lawyer."
    "Don't be stupid, Rosa. You're a smart girl. You can get a good job. Maybe you can be a secretary. That pays good."
    "But Poppy, I protested, I want to be a lawyer. I know I'm smart enough."
    "You're too smart for your father, eh? Too smart for this family? What we do isn't good enough for you?"
    "No, it's good enough, but I want to do better."
    He exploded. "You're gonna do better than me? Come over here, I'll beat the brains right out of you."

    Rosa

    A. Understatement
    B. Sentence length
    C. Hyperbole
    D. Metaphor

II. Writing Activity: Voice

For this assignment, read the paragraph below. A writer's voice is essential to lively writing. Remember, writers communicate voice by word choice, by sentence length and structure, by the subject, by the writer's attitude and approach, by the details, and by figurative language. This passage has little or no "voice" as a presence. Rewrite the passage, inserting your own voice, your presence. Use your imagination to add detail, similes, metaphors, attitude, and varied sentence length. If required, submit your revision to your instructor for evaluation.

> The writing group meets every Wednesday at 6:00 p.m. for coffee. Its members include Richard, Lakshmi, Rosa, Marcus, and Jada. When they meet, they discuss the weekly assignment and work together to assist each member with the week's assignment. This week, they are meeting to discuss an assignment about an event or memory from the past that had an effect on their individual lives. The instructor has informed them that writing is recursive and includes invention, delivery, and revision. The assignment is due the following Monday. They all wish to make a passing grade on the assignment.

III. Writing Activity: Punctuation

Punctuate the following dialogue between characters in the video. Remember to change paragraphs when you change speakers in addition to observing all the punctuation rules outlined in the Research and Writing chapter and the Rhetorical Handbook in your text. Place commas, periods, capital letters, exclamation points, quotes, hyphens, apostrophes, question marks, etc., in their appropriate place in the dialogue.

1. Did everyone bring something a memory for the first assignment

2. So who wants to go first it's my recipe for lamb vindaloo we only ate it on special occasions

3. What is the memory

4. The last time my mother cooked it was for the dinner the night before my wedding everybody was so happy I thought everything was perfect but then I tasted the curry and there was something different about it it had always tasted the same delicious and this time it wasn't right I should have known then that there was something wrong

5. Wow mine is a concert ticket third row center section Coldplay

6. Why was the concert important to you

_____
_____

7. The concert blew my mind musically but it also blew my mind in another sense I mean what I heard was amazing rock but what I felt was collective soul am I making any sense

_____
_____
_____

8. I brought a photograph taken last summer at my family reunion there are 122 members of my family in it most of whom I'd never met before

_____
_____
_____

9. Iraqi sand from Fallujah I spent 16 months over there and this is all I brought back this and a bunch of memories I'd rather forget

_____
_____
_____

10. Mine is a photo too of my quinceanera my fifteenth birthday don't I look happy it was the happiest day of my life

_____
_____

Lesson 1—Exploring the Process

ANSWER KEY

I. Writing Activity: Creating Voice

Answer	Learning Objectives	Focus Points	References
1. A	LO 4	FP 11	video segment 3; textbook, pp. 42–43
2. C, B	LO 4	FP 11	video segment 3; textbook, pp. 42–43
3. B	LO 4	FP 11	video segment 3; textbook, pp. 42–43

II. Writing Activity: Creating Voice

LO 4 ...... FP 2, 3, 7, 8, 9, 10, 11 .... video segments 3, 4; textbook, pp. 2–24, 786–788, 640–648, 778–785

(Your instructor will advise you about evaluating this assignment.)

III. Writing Activity: Punctuation

LO 5 ...... FP 3, 12 .... video segment 5; textbook, pp. 640–648, 664, 778–785

Correct punctuation for each question appears below.
(Please be aware that each passage may be punctuated in a variety of ways.)

1. "Did everyone bring something, a memory for the first assignment?"
2. "So, who wants to go first?"
   "It's my recipe for Lamb Vindaloo. We only ate it on special occasions."
3. "What is the memory?"
4. "The last time my mother cooked it was for the dinner the night before my wedding. Everybody was so happy. I thought everything was perfect, but then I tasted the curry. And, there was something different about it. It had always tasted the same: delicious, and this time it wasn't right. I should have known then that there was something wrong."
5. "Wow! Mine is a concert ticket, third row center section, *Coldplay*."
6. "Why was the concert important to you?"
7. "The concert blew my mind, musically, but it also blew my mind in another sense. I mean, what I heard was amazing rock, but what I felt was collective soul. Am I making any sense?"
8. "I brought a photograph taken last summer at my family reunion. There are 122 members of my family in it, most of whom I'd never met before."
9. "Iraqi sand from Fallujah. I spent 16 months over there, and this is all I brought back…this and a bunch of memories I'd rather forget."
10. "Mine is a photo of my *quinceanara*, my fifteenth birthday. Don't I look happy? It was the happiest day of my life!"

Lesson 1—Exploring the Process

Lesson 2

Explaining Relationships

Once the realization is accepted that even between the closest human beings infinite distances continue, a wonderful living side by side can grow, if they succeed in loving the distance between them which makes it possible for each to see the other whole against the sky.
—Rainer Maria Rilke

THEME

Writing about a relationship can lead to exciting discoveries. Perhaps the particular relationship you choose to describe will lead you to discover something poignant about its nature or help you to explore subtle connections that were not obvious at first. You might even discover a relationship where, initially, you thought none existed.

Relationships are everywhere, but examining a specific relationship sometimes presents a tricky mine field to wander through. In your journey of discovery, develop questions that help you avoid the "booby traps" imposed by conventional thinking. What are some unusual features of the relationship? Where is the relationship going? Why does he/she/it behave so strangely? Why can't the two entities understand each other?

When you write about a relationship, think about the significance of a particular kind of relationship, or explain how a particular relationship is similar to something else, or how a relationship reveals something important about a subject. Pursue the discovery of the relationship you plan to write about as an adventure and a journey into unknown dimensions. Doing so will make it possible for you to "see the other whole against the sky."

Piglet sidled up to Pooh from behind. "Pooh!" he whispered.
"Yes, Piglet?"
"Nothing," said Piglet, taking Pooh's paw. "I just wanted to be sure of you."
—A. A. Milne

LESSON RESOURCES

Textbook: Mauk and Metz: *The Composition of Everyday Life*
- Chapter 2, "Explaining Relationships," pp. 50–93
- Chapter 15, "Rhetorical Handbook"
  – "Verb," pp. 792–797
  – "Writing Style," pp. 754–756

Video: "Explaining Relationships" from the series *The Writer's Circle*

LESSON GOAL

You will communicate a discovery of the qualities of a relationship and the increased understanding of the existence of an undiscovered relationship in a narration or description.

LESSON LEARNING OBJECTIVES

1. Develop a thesis dealing with a particular relationship, past or present.
2. Apply organizational strategies to writing an analysis of the relationship, past or present.
3. Apply revision strategies to determine placement of the elements of the relationship essay.

LESSON FOCUS POINTS

1. What is involved in pre-writing when writing about a relationship?
2. What is involved in the analysis of a topic on relationships?
3. How is the main idea central to developing a thesis?
4. How does narration work in an essay about relationships?
5. How does description work in an essay about relationships?
6. How can a writer use figurative language (simile and metaphor) in an essay about relationships?
7. How should writers begin narrative or descriptive essays about relationships? Where should the thesis or main point go? What should writers include? When should writers change paragraphs? When should writers make transitions? How should writers conclude?
8. What are "writerly whispers"? What are "writerly yells"? How do these techniques draw the reader in closer and give emphasis in an essay about relationships?
9. What is "writerly pace"? What are the ways a writer can control speed and time in writing a narrative/descriptive essay about relationships?

WRITERS INTERVIEWED

Eric Jerome Dickey, Novelist, Los Angeles, CA
Laeta Kalogridis, Screenwriter, Encino, CA
John Phillip Santos, Author and Poet, San Antonio, TX

SUGGESTED WRITING ASSIGNMENTS

Consult with your instructor and the course syllabus about requirements for any of the assignments listed below.

1. Write a short multi-paragraph essay about a relationship using narration, description, figurative language, and/or analysis.
2. To practice narration, write down a *clean* joke that fully engages the reader through details and figurative language. (Use discretion in language and subject matter choices.)
3. To practice using descriptive details, add specific information to the following sentence: The girl walked into the room. Try to expand the sentence into a descriptive paragraph.
4. Discuss your topic with a friend. Start with the question, "Have you ever thought about the relationship between _____ and _____?" Write a memorandum to your instructor about your discussion. Explain how your understanding of the topic may have changed because of the discussion.
5. List three forms of delivery other than an essay that you might use to express your idea about a relationship (report, letter, screenplay, website, speech, song, poem, action). How might your message differ if delivered by way of these other forms?

Lots of people want to ride with you in the limo, but what you want is someone who will take the bus with you when the limo breaks down.
—Oprah Winfrey

ENRICHMENT ACTIVITIES

Complete the following activities. An answer key and/or guidelines appear at the end of this lesson for each activity.

I. Writing Activity: Writerly Pace

Having more details slows down time for the reader. In a film, time slows down when a writer (or director) focuses on particular details. On the other hand, having fewer details speeds up time for the reader. The fewer details a reader gets, the more quickly the reader moves through the events or thoughts in a text.

1. Rewrite the following passage from an essay in your textbook. Eliminate details in order to speed up time for the reader. If required, submit your revision to your instructor for evaluation.

   > I have a dog, or should I say, my dog has me. As I once explained to a non-dog owner, "Logan and I have a symbiotic relationship: I feed him, walk him, bathe him, take him to the vet, give him his heartworm and flea-and-tick medicines, buy him treats, pet him, and play with him. And what does he do? He lets me."
   >
   > "Dog-Tied" —David Hawes

2. Rewrite the following passage from an essay in your textbook. Add details in order to slow down time for the reader. If required, submit your revision to your instructor for evaluation.

   > Pity the doctor who thinks that prescribing a drug is the same thing as treating a patient, and the patient who agrees. Some never learn otherwise. The rest of us slowly wake up to the fact that the prescription is just the beginning, sometimes not even that.
   >
   > "We Love Them. We Hate Them. We Take Them." —Abigail Zuger

II. Writing Activity: Introductions

Review the information in your text on p. 84 about how to begin an essay about a relationship.
- You may begin with a general statement about a relationship.
- You may begin with a brief story or anecdote about the relationship.
- You may begin with a typical belief or stereotype about the relationship, and then turn to your own insight.
- You may begin with a fictional account, or scenario, of a relationship.

Rewrite the introductory paragraph, shown below, of Lakshmi's relationship essay using one of the techniques listed above. If required, submit your revision to your instructor for evaluation.

Something has come over me. I am no longer able to see only what is visible to the naked eye. Instead, wherever I go, I am aware of that which is too small to be seen. What I see, or what I sense, is the world of germs. There are billions upon billions of them, inhabiting every nook and cranny of the universe, and though I cannot actually see them, now that I know they're there I can't stop thinking about them. If there are billions of germs living inside of me, it seems to me that the safest thing to do is to be a good host.

_____
_____
_____
_____
_____
_____
_____
_____
_____
_____
_____
_____
_____
_____
_____
_____
_____

III. Writing Activity: Providing Support

Support the following generalizations from Lakshmi's essay with specific detail to give the reader a clear view of her explanation of the human relationship with germs. Use narration (storytelling), description (detail), and figurative language (metaphor and simile) in revising the statements. Use your imagination! If required, submit your revision to your instructor for evaluation.

1. They even kill other germs that threaten us.

2. In fact, the only time most of us consider our relationship to germs is when we're afraid of being infected by them.

3. We think of them as hostile little pests whose only goal is to harm us.

4. But the medical facts are a lot more complicated.

5. They are in the air, in the water, in the soil, on our food, on the surfaces we touch, and in every part of our bodies.

IV. Writing Activity: Conclusions

Rewrite Lakshmi's conclusion to her essay on our relationship with germs. Use one of the techniques described on page 86 of your textbook. If required, submit your revision to your instructor for evaluation.

- The overall statement on, and particular meaning of, the relationship (the thesis).
- An allusion that best illustrates your points about the relationship.
- A return to the introductory image or scene that reveals something significant about the image.

So, if we can't destroy germs, and we need them to survive, maybe we need to relate to them differently. Now that I know they're not out to get me, I'm going to work on having a better relationship with them. If there are billions of germs living inside of me, it seems to me that the safest thing to do is to be a good host.

ANSWER KEY

	Learning Objectives	Focus Points	References

I. Writing Activity: Writerly Pace
1. LO 2 .... FP 9 .... video segment 3; textbook, pp. 65, 89
2. LO 2 .... FP 9 .... video segment 3; textbook, pp. 59–60, 89

(Your instructor will advise you about evaluating this assignment.)

II. Writing Activity: Introductions
LO 2 .... FP 7 .... video segments 3, 4; textbook, p. 84

(Your instructor will advise you about evaluating this assignment.)

III. Writing Activity: Providing Support
LO 2 .... FP 4–6 .... video segments 3, 4; textbook, p. 90

(Your instructor will advise you about evaluating this assignment.)

IV. Writing Activity: Conclusions
LO 3 .... FP 7 .... video segments 3, 4; textbook, p. 86

(Your instructor will advise you about evaluating this assignment.)

Lesson 3

Observing Details

Art is born of the observation and investigation of Nature.
—Cicero (106 BC-43 BC)

THEME

For writers and students of writing, observation is an important tool. Observing is about discovery, finding something unique about a subject. Going beyond a casual glance, observers study their subjects and learn something by seeing them in particular ways, outside normal expectations and biases. Learning to observe involves learning how to see things and how to notice what is beneath the surface. Observers make general observations and then focus their perspective on a particular issue or subject and analyze the subject to find significance for their audience.

Discovering the unique characteristics of a subject and communicating them to an audience in sharp, particular detail are skills you will apply in writing an observation. You will observe places, people, animals, and objects and in those observations discover meaning that can be communicated to others. In detailing your observation, you will use narration, allusions, simile, and metaphor. When you revise your observation, you will discover the details that best convey your observational thesis and omit details that are unnecessary.

Where observation is concerned, chance favors only the prepared mind.
—Louis Pasteur

LESSON RESOURCES

Textbook: Mauk and Metz: *The Composition of Everyday Life*
- Chapter 3, "Observing," pp. 94–141
- Chapter 15, "Rhetorical Handbook"
  - "Organization," pp. 748–749
  - "Paragraphs," pp. 750–753
  - "Commas," pp. 778–782

Video: "Observing Details" from the series *The Writer's Circle*

LESSON GOAL

You will communicate an increase in your ability to observe details that lead to discovery of what lies beneath the first sight of a subject.

LESSON LEARNING OBJECTIVES

1. Observe a subject to discover specific details that would not be evident on first sight.
2. Use rhetorical strategies (i.e., arrangement of details) to communicate the observation of a subject in specific terms.
3. Revise the observation focusing on the writer's voice (active, passive, present, or invisible "I").

LESSON FOCUS POINTS

1. How does a writer find a subject to observe? A place? A person? An animal?
2. What constitutes analysis in writing an observation?
3. What are observation notes?
4. What questions should a writer ask while observing?
5. How does a writer articulate a thesis about a subject of an observation?
6. How does a writer use narrative in an observation?
7. How are allusions useful in an observation?
8. How are simile and metaphor useful in an observation?
9. How does a writer determine public resonance about the topic of an observation? Why does this topic matter to others?
10. How does a writer select and arrange details in an essay of observation?
11. When should the writer change paragraphs in an observation?
12. What is the present "I" and how is it used in an observation essay? The invisible "I"?
13. What are levels of formality? How do levels of formality affect the audience of an observation essay?

WRITERS INTERVIEWED

Jenny Anmuth, Travel Editor, Frommer's Travel Guides, South Salem, NY
Naomi Shihab Nye, Author and Poet, San Antonio, TX

SUGGESTED WRITING ASSIGNMENT

Consult with your instructor and the course syllabus about requirements for the assignment listed below.

Write an essay of observation with details that lead the reader to the discovery of what lies beneath the first sight of a subject.

There are three principal means of acquiring knowledge...observation of nature, reflection, and experimentation. Observation collects facts; reflection combines them; experimentation verifies the result of that combination.
—Denis Diderot

ENRICHMENT ACTIVITIES

Complete the following activities. Guidelines or an answer key appear at the end of this lesson.

I. Writing Activity: Using Commas
Insert or delete commas where appropriate in this excerpt from an interview with poet, Naomi Shihab Nye. Check the answer key for one way to insert commas. If required, submit to your instructor for evaluation.

My advice to writers of any age about beginning as a writer and we all do in some ways we're always beginning is to read widely because if you read widely many styles of writing many different voices you may find someone who really speaks to you. So begin with reading widely and asking yourself what is this voice doing with words on the page that I appreciate? How is it happening? And then write on a regular basis would be my second piece of advice. It doesn't have to be long chunks of writing. Even five minutes a day can revolutionize your own relationship with your own writing. But the regularity can be very helpful to a beginning writer because you get into a pace a rhythm. You have a body of material developing in little increments day by day and then find some way to share your work whether with one friend or a class or a literary magazine on your campus or at a coffee house.

Those would be the three suggestions I make most commonly to beginning writers.

Naomi Shihab Nye

II. **Writing Activity: Creating Vitality**
Add specific details from your own imagination to these excerpts from Jada's essay to support her observation. If required, submit your detailed response to your instructor for evaluation.

> I never had a dog when I was growing up. In the army they made me an MP and I was handling dogs a lot, and I liked that part. One thing I like about dogs is that they give to you just what you give to them.
>
> They were going to do a longer search the next day, for the advanced dogs. I wish I could have gone with them. It was fun watching the dogs train and just being with them. I think they enjoyed it, too. It's like they have a job and I think a lot of dogs want a job. In that way, they are a lot like me.

III. **Writing Activity: "Invisible vs. Present I"**
Revise these passages to omit or add "I" (invisible or present). Which passage is more appealing, yours or the writer's? Explain how the present or invisible "I" adds or subtracts from your voice or the writer's voice. If required, submit your response to your instructor for evaluation.

> I was relaxed on the tree trunk, ensconced in the lap of lichen, watching the lily pads at my feet tremble and part dreamily over the thrusting path of a carp. A yellow bird appeared to my right and flew behind me. It caught my eye; I swiveled around…and the next instant, inexplicably, I was looking down at a weasel, who was looking up at me.

Annie Dillard

_____
_____
_____
_____
_____
_____
_____
_____

Some twenty-five chimpanzees were regularly visiting camp by then, and there had been more than enough work for all of the staff. After watching the chimps all day, the staff had often transcribed notes from tape recorders until late at night.

                                                                               Jane Goodall

_____
_____
_____
_____
_____
_____
_____
_____

The front porch fell victim to its two natural enemies: the internal-combustion engine (automobiles) and electricity (air conditioning, lights, and TV). Now, instead of gathering on the front porch as their grandparents did, McCovey's family are either gone somewhere thanks to transportation or they are at home but indoors.

                                                                          Chester McCovey

_____
_____
_____
_____
_____
_____
_____
_____

IV. Writing Activity: Structure and Organization of an Essay

Look at Jada's first draft of her essay and review page 749. Outline the essay by identifying the controlling idea and the topic of each supporting paragraph. When you finish your outline, write a **brief** explanation of areas where you had difficulty. How might this exercise help you in drafting other essays for this course? If required, submit your response to your instructor for evaluation.

Jada's Essay Draft

Yesterday, on Saturday, I went to a dog training session for search and rescue dogs. It was at the end of a long road with a fence, behind were the dogs barking really loud when I got there.

The dogs were trying real hard to do all the things the handlers wanted them to. The first part was all obedience things. Like heeling, and sitting and staying. It is hard for the dogs because they were supposed to sit and stay without being able to see their handler for five minutes. And then they were supposed to stay down from fifteen yards away. Some of the dogs were not good at that. I think because they were so excitable. Next came the agility course, which looked real fun for the dogs. The dogs had to do all sorts of obstacles. Like windows. And on a balance beam. The handler was running next to the dog, telling them where to go, but only with their hands. They couldn't talk to the dogs. Only signals. The dogs were leaping and running and some of them I thought were smiling.

I never had a dog when I was growing up. In the army they made me an MP and I was handling dogs a lot, and I liked that part. One thing I like about dogs is that they give to you just what you give to them.

The most hard part of the search part was sniffing, or tracking. This is like when a dog has to try to find a person. At the Kimball course they try and mess with the dog, by making it only have a few things to sniff. A dog can smell a lot better than a person. They said that a dog had 125 million olfactory cells, and a person only has like 5 million. I was impressed thinking about that, how good the dog can smell better than me. An olfactory cell is what you have in your nose. The other thing they said about the dog is that when he is sniffing, he is always right. They called that "believing in your dog." After what I saw, with one dog sniffing a track over rocks, I believe it.

The dogs also had to do retrieving. They went and got stuff from the person they were supposed to find, which was left out for them. One dog just looked up in the air, and his nose was twitching, and then he shot off like a bullet until he was pulling out a piece of a shirt on the trail. I couldn't even see the piece of that shirt when I was standing there, and he could smell it and then goes and finds it. It was amazing.

They were going to do a longer search the next day, which was supposed to be for the advanced dogs. I wish I could have gone with them. It was pretty fun being with all those dogs, watching them and just being with them. They are pretty happy, I think. It's like they have a job and I think a lot of dogs want a job.

ANSWER KEY

	Learning	Focus	
Answer	Objectives	Points	References

I. Writing Activity: Using Commas
............LO 2, 3.............FP 10..textbook, pp. 778–782

My advice to writers of any age about beginning as a writer, and we all do in some ways, we're always beginning, is to read widely because if you read widely many styles of writing, many different voices, you may find someone who really speaks to you. So begin with reading widely and asking yourself, what is this voice doing with words on the page that I appreciate? How is it happening? And, then, write on a regular basis would be my second piece of advice. It doesn't have to be long chunks of writing. Even five minutes a day can revolutionize your own relationship with your own writing. But the regularity can be very helpful to a beginning writer because you get into a pace, a rhythm. You have a body of material developing in little increments day by day, and then find some way to share your work, whether with one friend or a class or a literary magazine on your campus or at a coffee house. Those would be the three suggestions I make most commonly to beginning writers.

*Commas are configured in a variety of ways, so there may be numerous possibilities for punctuating this passage.

II. Writing Activity: Creative Vitality
............LO 2, 3............FP 6–8, 10..video segment 2; textbook, pp. 136–137
(Your instructor will advise you about evaluating this assignment.)

III. Writing Activity: "Invisible vs. Present I"
1. ....LO 3...................FP 12.....................................video segment 5; textbook, pp. 98–100, 133
2. ....LO 3...................FP 12.....................................video segment 5; textbook, pp. 104–110, 33
3. ....LO 3...................FP 12.....................................video segment 5; textbook, pp. 115–116, 133

IV. Writing Activity: Structure and Organization in an Essay
...............LO 2.................FP 2–11.. video segments 4, 6; textbook, p. 749
(Your instructor will advise you about evaluating this assignment.)

Lesson 4

Analyzing Concepts

Analysis is more likely to adjust evidence than to adjust itself.
—Mason Cooley

THEME

In this lesson, specific and detailed information about analysis and about concepts appears for your examination. After you spend time reading and digesting that information, your assignment is to examine a concept, defined as an idea or abstract formulation that is specific and open to change and variation. Concepts can sometimes be defined as "moving targets" that might even differ drastically within a particular culture. Since concepts are not always agreed upon, dispute over a concept is often the driving force behind major armed conflicts between people, cultures, and countries. For example, Viet Nam, Korea, Iran, Iraq, Israel, and Russia, all experienced disputes and disagreements about the concepts and ideologies which drive the people within their own countries. As history indicates, civil war often results when citizens cannot agree on particular concepts. Concepts about topics like God, man, woman, family, or life have all brought on intense, highly publicized legal battles in America as well as other countries. Individuals struggle with personal concepts as well, particularly students who are exploring the transition to adulthood. Obviously, concepts are emotionally charged, and the analysis of concepts leading to different points of view create conflict: armed, legal, academic, and personal.

    In your college pursuits, you may encounter the fact that concepts often differ from discipline to discipline. Family, for example, is perceived differently in biology, sociology, psychology, anthropology, and literature. A discipline's definition of a concept aids in defining the discipline in academic battles. As a student writer, once you identify a concept, further steps will be necessary to analyze the concept or discover its meaning. The strategies you learn in this chapter will help you investigate the particular parts, elements, or ideas within the whole. As you will see in the video, a good analysis dismantles the whole concept and shows meaning inside the individual elements. In your own written analysis, you must create a bridge between your concept and the surrounding world.

The poem, like any human being, is something more than its most complete analysis. Like any human being, it gives a sense of unified individuality.
—Donald Stauffer

LESSON RESOURCES

Textbook: Mauk and Metz: *The Composition of Everyday Life*
- Chapter 4, "Analyzing Concepts," pp. 142–187
- Chapter 15, "Rhetorical Handbook"
  - "Sentence Vitality," pp. 757–760
  - "Coherence and Conciseness," pp. 761–764
  - "Complete Sentences," pp. 765–767
  - "Commas," pp. 778–782

Video: "Analyzing Concepts" from the series *The Writer's Circle*

LESSON GOAL

You will communicate the understanding of a concept in the everyday world through analysis and communication of the ideas that lie beyond the concept by practicing the processes of invention, delivery, and revision.

LESSON LEARNING OBJECTIVES

1. Select a particular concept to analyze in writing.
2. Practice various organizational strategies for writing about the concept.
3. Use the revision process to verify that the analysis of the concept is clear, understandable, and relevant.
4. Use the peer review process to avoid common sentence errors.

LESSON FOCUS POINTS

1. How does a writer go about finding a concept to analyze at work, school, church, or home? In activities like sports events, concerts, official meetings, and community events?
2. How does an analysis of the key concepts within a student's major assist in analyzing concepts? How does watching television programs or reading advertisements in magazines and on billboards assist in finding key hidden concepts?
3. What questions serve as aids to analysis for writers?
4. How does a writer discover if the concept chosen for analysis matters to others?
5. How does the writer analyzing a concept develop ideas? Discover a thesis? Develop supporting paragraphs?
6. When analyzing a concept, what questions are useful to a writer in developing supporting ideas?
7. How may a writer use definitions in analyzing a concept? How are dictionary definitions helpful or not helpful?
8. How may a writer use outside sources in analyzing a concept?

9. How does a writer analyzing a concept begin the essay? Work ideas into the essay? Change paragraphs? Determine placement of the thesis? Conclude the essay?
10. How does a writer use metaphor in an essay analyzing a concept?
11. What revision strategies are helpful to the writer of an analysis of a concept essay?

WRITERS INTERVIEWED

Carol Berkin, Historian and Author, Baruch College, City University of New York, New York, NY

Richard Rodriguez, Essayist and Journalist, San Francisco, CA

SUGGESTED WRITING ASSIGNMENTS

Consult with your instructor and the course syllabus about requirements for any of the assignments listed below.

1. Write an essay in which you analyze a particular concept with the purpose of enhancing the understanding of the reader.
2. Write a memo to your instructor explaining why the main idea of your essay is significant. Your memo should touch on the essay's public resonance and how it might affect a reader's thinking or behavior.
3. Find an image that relates to your essay, and write a caption for the image. Then write an explanation of the relationship between your image and your text. Next show the image to several people and ask each person to read your essay. Then ask them how they view the original image differently.

Literature is analysis after the event.
—Doris Lessing

ENRICHMENT ACTIVITIES

Complete the following activities. An answer key and/or guidelines appear at the end of this lesson for each activity.

I. Writing Activity: Avoiding Sentence Errors (Fragments, Comma Splices, and Run-ons)

Read the following passages taken from Rosa's essay in Lesson Four of the course video. The passages contain major sentence errors. Identify each error: fragment, comma splice, or run-on sentence by circling the correct answer. Then, rewrite the sentence to correct it in the space provided.

- Fragments are incomplete sentences and usually do not contain a subject or a verb. Example: Going into town.
- Comma splices are two complete sentences connected only by a comma. Comma splices leave out coordinating conjunctions (and, or, nor, yet, but, for, or so). Example: Esther and Joseph went to town, they came home by way of Perry's house.
- Run-on sentences are two complete sentences with no punctuation or coordinating conjunctions. Example: Sarah finished her college studies she then went to graduate school in Hawaii.

1. Really, the examples are too numerous. Except for the antacid ads.
   A. Fragment
   B. Comma splice
   C. Run-on sentence

   Revision: _____
   _____

2. In the ads, they are all young and thin, their hair is soft and shiny, their cheekbones are sculpted.
   A. Fragment
   B. Comma splice
   C. Run-on sentence

   Revision: _____
   _____
   _____

Lesson 4—Analyzing Concepts

3. Usually just making breakfast, a long, boring commute through traffic, and days filled with endless legal briefs to read.
   A. Fragment
   B. Comma splice
   C. Run-on sentence

   Revision: _____

4. You would think that if someone were trying to sell me something, they would sell me something that relates to my life they sell me endless fantasy, almost always beyond my reach and frequently beyond my comprehension.
   A. Fragment
   B. Comma splice
   C. Run-on sentence

   Revision: _____

5. It's not like I want someone to sell me my life. At least not the life that is on the surface.
   A. Fragment
   B. Comma splice
   C. Run-on sentence

   Revision: _____

6. I wish there were a beauty for the rest of us. A beauty not based on hourglass figures and wrinkle free smiles lit with perfect teeth but on flabby imperfect bodies.
   A. Fragment
   B. Comma splice
   C. Run-on sentence

   Revision: _____

Lesson 4—Analyzing Concepts

7. And, wouldn't it be great if that kind of beauty showed up in the ads people were more interested in seeing themselves for who they really were, rather than for something they can never be?
   A. Fragment
   B. Comma splice
   C. Run-on sentence

   Revision: _____
   _____
   _____

8. But it feels like everything they are selling is really for someone else, not the ordinary people I see lined up with their ordinary kids at an ordinary grocery store. And certainly not for me.
   A. Fragment
   B. Comma splice
   C. Run-on sentence

   Revision: _____
   _____
   _____

II. Writing Activity: Stilted Language

Stilted language consists of an overly elaborate and unnecessarily elevated jungle of clauses and phrases. Stilted language presents vague ideas stretched out over unnecessary phrases. Stilted language jumbles ideas so that readers are left guessing or wondering, and it inflates ideas so that they seem beyond exploration.

Rewrite the following passage to eliminate stilted language. If required, submit your response to your instructor.

> In higher education, principles establish how a discipline works. Composition works on principles and conventions of grammar and persuasion. This is not to say that all knowledge is prescribed. On the contrary, students in such classes are encouraged to invent, to break rules, to go beyond. But in order to do so, they need certain ground rules; they need to understand that certain principles exist in the world outside of their own desires.
>
> *Have It Your Way: Consumerism Invades Education*
> —Simon Benlow

III. Writing Activity: Adding Zest to Your Writing

Find several lifeless sentences from one of your previous essays. Bring those sentences to life. Make sure that your new, more vital sentences are clear, concise, coherent, and complete. Make them shorter, not longer than their lifeless predecessors if you can. If required, submit both the lifeless sentences and the revisions to your instructor.

IV. Writing Activity: Concept Analysis

As you look closely at the concept you have identified to analyze for this lesson, write answers to the following questions. If required, submit your responses to your instructor:

- Specifically, how does the concept influence or change people's lives?
- What particular emotions or ideas are associated with the concept?
- What specific responsibilities come with it?
- What hidden role does it play in everyday life?
- Are there complexities to the concept that people overlook?

ANSWER KEY

I. Writing Activity: Avoiding Sentence Errors (Fragments, Comma Splices, and Run-ons)
(Numerous possibilities exist for the revision of the sentences. What follows are possible revisions.)

Answer	Learning Objectives	Focus Points	References

1. A .... LO 4 .... FP 11 .... textbook, pp. 765–767
   Really, the examples are too numerous, except for the antacid ads.

2. B .... LO 4 .... FP 11 .... textbook, pp. 765–767
   In the ads, they are all young and thin. Their hair is soft and shiny. Their cheekbones are sculpted.

3. A .... LO 4 .... FP 11 .... textbook, pp. 765–767
   Usually, I just make breakfast and endure a long, boring commute through traffic. My days are filled with endless legal briefs to read.

4. C .... LO 4 .... FP 11 .... textbook, pp. 765–767
   You would think that if someone were trying to sell me something, they would sell me something that relates to my life. They sell me endless fantasy, almost always beyond my reach and frequently beyond my comprehension.

5. A .... LO 4 .... FP 11 .... textbook, pp. 765–767
   It's not like I want someone to sell me my life, at least not the life that is on the surface.

6. A .... LO 4 .... FP 11 .... textbook, pp. 765–767
   I wish there were a beauty for the rest of us. I wish there were a beauty not based on hourglass figures and wrinkle free smiles lit with perfect teeth but on flabby imperfect bodies.

	Learning	Focus	
Answer	Objectives	Points	References

7. C ....LO 4 ....FP 11 ....textbook, pp. 765–767
   And, wouldn't it be great if that kind of beauty showed up in the ads? Wouldn't it be great if people were more interested in seeing themselves for who they really were, rather than something they can never be?

8. A ....LO 4 ....FP 11 ....textbook, pp. 765–767
   But it feels like everything they are selling is really for someone else, not the ordinary people I see lined up with their ordinary kids at an ordinary grocery store. And, it is certainly not for me.

II. Writing Activity: Stilted Language
...............LO 3 ....FP 11 ....video segment 3; textbook pp. 142–187
(Your instructor will advise you about evaluating this assignment.)

III. Writing Activity: Adding Zest to Your Writing
...............LO 4 ....FP 11 ....textbook, pp. 182–183, 757–760, 761–764
(Your instructor will advise you about evaluating this assignment.)

IV. Writing Activity: Concept Analysis
...............LO 2, 3 ....FP 2, 3, 4, 7, 8, 10 .... video segments 1, 2, 5, 6; textbook, pp. 142–187
(Your instructor will advise you about evaluating this assignment.)

Lesson 5

Analyzing Images

I saw the angel in the marble and carved until I set him free.
—Michelangelo

THEME

You see a constant barrage of images on a daily basis: posters, signs, advertisements, television, billboards, book covers, sculpture, photographs, and the Internet to name just a few. Analyzing, comprehending, and interpreting those images is probably not something you are accustomed to doing. The meaning of any image is varied and transitory in itself. Add to that the individual thought processes of each viewer, and you have a myriad of responses.

In this lesson, you will select an image that attracts you for whatever reason. Using the tools provided in the text and the video, you will analyze that image closely to try to understand its relationship to you and to your classmates and to anyone who might view that image. The video lesson provides one student's analysis of the Nike Swoosh. Hopefully, the image will provide an impetus and encouragement to your imaginative self in inventive thinking and intensive writing. As you investigate, look beyond and behind the obvious and pay particular attention to the details of the image and its meaning to the audience as well as its impact on the culture it exemplifies.

The man who has no imagination has no wings.
—Muhammad Ali

LESSON RESOURCES

Textbook: Mauk and Metz: *The Composition of Everyday Life*
- Chapter 5, "Analyzing Images," pp. 188–243
- Chapter 15, "Rhetorical Handbook"
  - "Beyond the Five-Paragraph Essay," p. 749
  - "Coherence and Conciseness," pp. 761–764
  - "Organization," p. 748
  - "Colons," p. 782

Video: "Analyzing Images" from the series *The Writer's Circle*

LESSON GOAL

You will increase your understanding of explaining how the elements of an image work to impact the feelings and consciousness of the viewers.

LESSON LEARNING OBJECTIVES

1. Select a particular image to analyze in writing.
2. Explain how the visual elements of the image affect the viewer's perception.
3. Analyze the relationship of the image to viewers in terms of text, subtext, and context.
4. Edit the language of an essay to improve its intensity and coherence.

LESSON FOCUS POINTS

1. How does a writer select an image for analysis? What value does the writer gain from seeing inside the workings of images? How do writers become sophisticated readers of images?
2. How does a writer break down an image to understand how it works, how it conveys meaning, and how it conceals values and beliefs? What is involved in analyzing an image?
3. How do the elements of an image convey ideas and feelings? Work on the consciousness of the viewer? Speak to a surrounding culture? Resonate with surrounding values and beliefs?
4. What is content in an image? Framing? Composition? Focus? Lighting? Texture? Angle and Vantage Point? Significance?
5. How is meaning generated by the interaction of image and text?
6. What is intertextuality? How does it add layers of meaning to any text?
7. What is subtext? What is implication in subtext?
8. Explain the subtext of images. What subtle assumptions or beliefs are suggested by or lurking in an image?
9. What is context? What is specific context? What is cultural context?
10. Why should writers keep developing nuances and asking more questions about images?
11. What is an invention workshop? How does it work?
12. Why is the thesis important in the analysis of an image? Why is it important to focus on a particular element in a thesis about analyzing an image? Why is it important to provide an explanation of the significance of the particular element?
13. What are the two general categories for support in analyzing images? Why are details from the image useful in developing support for the thesis? Why is it helpful to use evidence like cultural allusions in supporting a thesis?
14. How can research be helpful in analyzing an image? When should a writer use headings? How should a writer integrate outside sources?

15. How does a writer create intensity? What is pitch in writing intensity? How does a writer use the personal to analyze?
16. What is vitality? How does a writer prune language in an essay? What is blueprinting and how can a writer avoid it?
17. What are vague pronouns? How can a writer avoid vague pronouns?
18. What is peer review? Describe a process for peer review.
19. What is collaboration? How is it useful in analyzing an image?

WRITERS INTERVIEWED

Jenny Anmuth, Travel Editor and Writer, Frommer's Travel Guides, South Salem, NY
Matt Zoller Seitz, Film and Television Critic, *New York Press/Newark Star Ledger,* Brooklyn, NY

SUGGESTED WRITING ASSIGNMENTS

Consult with your instructor and the course syllabus about requirements for any of the assignments listed below.

1. Draft an essay of analysis on a particular image based on a focused point and specific support strategies that show its relationship to the viewer of the image.
2. Write about a particular image (type of image or group of images) that is a "signpost" pointing people in the wrong direction. Write a focused thesis and support it with strategies that illuminate how the image(s) point others in the wrong direction. Convince your audience that the image is "negative."
3. Analyze an effective advertising image that uses illogical appeals. Why is the lack of logic ignored by the public?

It is the eye of ignorance that assigns a fixed and unchangeable color to every object; beware of this stumbling block.
—Paul Gauguin

ENRICHMENT ACTIVITIES

Complete the following activities. An answer key and/or guidelines appear at the end of this lesson for each activity.

I. Writing Activity: Intensity in Voice

Read the following passage taken from a draft of Marcus' essay on the Nike Swoosh. Rewrite the passage to create intensity, to insist that the reader pay attention. Use repetition, parenthetical phrases, and word choice. If required, submit your response to your instructor for evaluation.

1. In addition to its visual elements, the Swoosh also gathers meaning from the words and images with which it is associated. By pairing the logo with a no-nonsense command, the well-known "Just Do It" ad campaign drives home its message of speed, simplicity, and power. The out-of the ordinary message that the Swoosh transmits is reinforced by its familiar presence on the clothes of athletes like Michael Jordan and Tiger Woods. Complicating this perception is the widespread campaign to discredit Nike for its exploitive third world labor practices and to persuade top celebrities to reject the Swoosh as their emblem.

II. Writing Activity: Blueprinting

Identify examples of "blueprinting" in the following passages from Marcus' essay. "Blueprinting" gives the reader information that draws attention to the writer's plans. The writers tell the reader what they are doing and/or what they are about to do. Rewrite the sentences so that the writer states his points rather than announcing his plans. With the blueprinting removed, a sentence can hold more information. If required, submit your responses to your instructor for evaluation.

1. What is it in this seemingly simple image that carries so much weight? This is the question I will examine in the following paragraphs.

2. To summarize my analysis of the Nike Swoosh, the image is clean and simple with a strong sense of motion, even speed.

III. Writing Activity: Colons

Colons are useful for connecting a list, explanation, or quotation to the statement introducing it. Use a colon in a sentence only after you express a complete thought. Rewrite these passages from a draft of Marcus' essay. Insert colons where necessary and delete unnecessary colons. Check the answer key at the end of this lesson for possible answers.

1. At first glance, the content of the Swoosh is nothing special: just a curved stripe in a field of color.

2. For instance: the low angle from which it is presented gives it a feeling of power.

3. This sense of motion is amplified by the framing of the Swoosh: it is most often found in an empty field, with nothing else near it, giving it an air of limitless potential.

    _____
    _____
    _____

4. It comes in many different colors, depending on the color of the item on which it appears this gives it an almost organic quality, as though it is an inherent part of the object to which it is affixed.

    _____
    _____
    _____
    _____

IV. Writing Activity: Intertextuality

Examine *The Writer's Circle* image below in terms of intertextuality. Then answer the following questions:

1. How does the text correlate with the significance of the image?
2. How do content, framing, composition, focus, lighting, texture, angle, and vantage point help to convey the ideas?
3. Does the text echo other texts? How does the language depend on our familiarity with other texts?
4. What seems to be the main idea of the image?
5. Besides the obvious statements or ideas, what subtle assumptions or beliefs are suggested by (or lurking in) the image?

If required, submit your responses to your instructor for evaluation.

ANSWER KEY

	Learning	Focus	
Answer	Objectives	Points	References

I. Writing Activity: Intensity in Voice
................LO 4 ....FP 15, 16, 17............................ video segments 2, 4, 6; textbook, pp. 238–241
(Your instructor will advise you about evaluating of this assignment.)

II. Writing Activity: Blueprinting
................LO 4 ....FP 16..video segment 5; textbook, p. 240
(Your instructor will advise you about evaluating this assignment.)

III. Writing Activity: Colons
(Numerous possibilities exist for the revision of the sentences. What follows are possible revisions.)

1. ....LO 4 ....FP 18, 19...p. 782
At first glance, the content of the Swoosh is nothing special, just a curved stripe in a field of color.

2. ....LO 4 ....FP 18, 19...p. 782
For instance, the low angle from which it is presented gives it a feeling of power.

3. ....LO 4 ....FP 18, 19...p. 782
This sense of motion is amplified by the framing of the Swoosh: it is most often found in an empty field, with nothing else near it, giving it an air of limitless potential.

4. ....LO 4 ....FP 18, 19...p. 782
It comes in many different colors, depending on the color of the item on which it appears: this gives it an almost organic quality, as though it is an inherent part of the object to which it is affixed.

IV. Writing Activity: Intertextuality
..............LO 2, 3 ....FP 2–6.................................. video segments 5, 6, 7; textbook, pp. 228–229
(Your instructor will advise you about evaluating this assignment.)

Lesson 5—Analyzing Images

Lesson 6

Building Arguments

Wars are poor chisels for carving out peaceful tomorrows.
—Dr. Martin Luther King, Jr.

THEME

In one way or another, you are surrounded by argument every day. You and your best friend might disagree about which restaurant you will choose for today's lunch; television and radio talk shows provide fodder for arguments; biologists argue about stem cell research and its appropriateness; psychologists argue about Freudian theory; and advertisers argue that their product is best. In your college courses and activities, argument is everywhere. Argument is the art of persuading people how to think through speeches, debates, and informal discussions. In all situations, arguers who can deliver the most sophisticated and engaging arguments tend to have the most influence. Argument is the key to vigorous, thoughtful writing for students who wish to succeed in their college courses.

Persuading an audience about how to think about a particular topic and employing a variety of strategies in convincing the audience are at the core of this lesson. Objectivity, analysis, explanation, and narration are all strategic to the success of any argument. You will deliver an argument to encourage new ways of thinking about your particular topic. In the course of the argument, you will explain how your claims relate to and differ from those of others.

The key to all of this is how you present your argument. You must win over the opposition with your own objectivity about the topic. Great arguers put personal biases and opinions aside in their search for objectivity. Use facts, statistics, data, real life experiences and events to prove your argument. And, of course, you must give credit to the opposing argument. In this lesson, you will learn the skills to provide an objective and convincing argument.

If you are going to tell people the truth, you had better make them laugh or they will kill you.

—Oscar Wilde

LESSON RESOURCES

Textbook: Mauk and Metz, *The Composition of Everyday Life*
- Chapter 6, "Making Arguments." pp. 244–301

Video: "Building Arguments" from the series *The Writer's Circle*

LESSON GOAL

Following the argumentative processes outlined in this lesson, you will employ a variety of rhetorical strategies to communicate increased persuasive skills in convincing an audience to think differently about a topic.

LESSON LEARNING OBJECTIVES

1. Write an arguable thesis statement with a specific claim.
2. Support the arguable thesis with evidence, appeals, and logic.
3. Revise drafts using rhetorical strategies that strengthen the argumentative position.

LESSON FOCUS POINTS

1. How does a writer discover an argumentative topic?
2. How does a writer analyze a topic to explore what it means and why it matters to the writer and others?
3. What is the arguable point of an argument? What is the main claim/thesis? What are some common thesis problems in writing an argument?
4. What is public resonance? What is scope? What is arguability?
5. What are the various kinds of evidence? How does a writer develop evidence to support an argumentative essay?
6. What are the various kinds of appeals? How does a writer use appeals in an essay?
7. What is counterargument? How do writers use counterargument to develop their points? How do writers use counterargument to qualify the thesis?
8. What is concession? How does a writer make concessions?
9. What are logical fallacies?
10. How should a writer begin an argument? How should a writer organize evidence in an argument? Where should the writer place counterarguments? How should the writer make transitions?
11. Why is it important to avoid harsh descriptions? Why should writers avoid character slams and preaching problems? Why is it important for writers to talk with, not argue at readers?
12. What revision strategies are helpful in writing arguments?

WRITERS INTERVIEWED

Macarena Hernandez, Editorial Columnist, *The Dallas Morning News*, Dallas, TX
Richard Rodriguez, Essayist and Journalist, San Francisco, CA

SUGGESTED WRITING ASSIGNMENTS

Consult with your instructor and the course syllabus about requirements for any of the assignments listed below.

1. Write an essay in which you argue for or against a particular point, convincing your readers that you have a new way of thinking about the topic with your analysis of the views of others and a thorough explanation of your claims related to the views of others.
2. Write a letter to the editor of either a local or national newspaper, expressing your main idea and support. Since you are sending your letter to a newspaper to be read by the general public, your letter must have clear public resonance.
3. Write a fake letter to an editor, but be certain that your letter has no public resonance. Notice how odd such a letter would be. Why would a newspaper not publish such a letter?

Truth needs no laws to enforce it.
—Michael Rivero

ENRICHMENT ACTIVITIES

Complete the following activities. An answer key and/or guidelines appear at the end of this lesson for each activity.

I. Writing Activity: Support Strategies and Appeals
Read the following passages and identify the support strategies and types of appeals from the choices listed after each passage. Circle all that apply for each passage. Check the answer key for possible responses.

1. Historically, mid-management positions in large corporations provided good incomes and considerable job security.

   David Crabtree, Ph.D.

   A. Scenarios
   B. Allusions
   C. Appeal to need
   D. Statistics

Lesson 6—Building Arguments
47

2. Fat people are assumed to be lazy, stupid, ugly, lacking in self-esteem and pride, devoid of self-control, and stuffed full of a host of other unpleasant qualities that have nothing to do with the size of a person's belly or thighs.

   Ann Marie Paulin

   A. Authorities
   B. Appeal to emotion
   C. Examples
   D. Facts

3. Think about the real situation of American Indians. Think about Julius Streicher. Remember Justice Jackson's admonition. Understand that the treatment of Indians in American popular culture is not "cute" or "amusing," or just "good, clean fun."

   Ward Churchill

   A. Appeal to value
   B. Personal testimonies
   C. Statistics
   D. Allusions

4. I've been lucky enough to have gained some wisdom (as well as weight) with age: I may be fat, but I'm no longer crazy. There are some things more important than being thin.

   Ann Marie Paulin

   A. Scenarios
   B. Appeal of character
   C. Authorities
   D. Appeal to logic

5. A recent study published by *Health Affairs* reported that three-quarters of the respondents who saw a drug on TV and asked their doctors for it were successful.

   Therese Cherry

   A. Allusions
   B. Statistics
   C. Appeal of character
   D. Examples

6. Psychologist Mary Pipher, in her book *Hunger Pains: The Modern Woman's Quest for Thinness*, cites a 1994 study which found that "90 percent of dieters regain all the weight they lost within five years."

   Ann Marie Paulin

   A. Authorities
   B. Statistics
   C. Appeal to logic
   D. Personal testimonies

II. Writing Activity: Counterargument

Develop a counterargument to this paragraph from Rosa's essay. (Counterarguments anticipate and refute claims or positions that oppose those forwarded by the writer.)

- List three possible support strategies or appeals that you might use in the counterargument.
- Begin the counterargument with one of the following transitional phrases: on the other hand, contrary to this idea, although many people take this stance, however, despite the evidence for this position, but.
- Use one of the support strategies and/or appeals from the list of questions on page 285 in your text.
- Pay attention to voice in order to avoid harshness and preachiness in the counterargument. This could possibly produce a turnabout paragraph.
- If required, submit your response to your instructor for evaluation.

> A recent study done by professors at Southside Virginia Community College found that statistically non-traditional students average a half grade point higher than traditional students. That's enough to turn a C student into a B student. Their study reinforces what many earlier studies had already concluded: that in a variety of tests in a variety of fields, nontraditional students make better grades than younger students.

III. Writing Activity: Revision

Rewrite the following paragraph from Rosa's essay in order to add support. Incorporate and make note of at least three rhetorical tools in your revision. (Rhetorical tools include examples, allusions, personal testimonies/anecdotes, scenarios, statistics, authorities, facts, appeals to logic, emotion, character, need, and value.) If required, submit your response to your instructor for evaluation.

> In addition, the professors in the Virginia study concluded that non-traditional students tended to bring to college the very qualities that would naturally lead to a better academic performance: motivation, maturity, life experience, and persistence. And doesn't that make sense? You know older students are motivated because they have chosen college. And someone who has a job, has raised kids, wouldn't you expect that person to have more maturity than a younger student with none of that experience? And persistence, that again is something you need in college and you would expect from an older student, who knows what it takes to achieve goals?

IV. Writing Activity: Logical Fallacies

Analyze popular advertisements from magazines, television, and the Internet for logical fallacies. Provide examples from at least three logical fallacies discussed in your textbook: ad hominem, strawperson, faulty cause/effect, either/or reasoning, hasty generalization, non sequitur, oversimplification, slippery slope, false analogy, and begging the question. For example: She attracts men by wearing Goddess perfume. I'm going to buy some because I want to be attractive to men as well. (Hasty Generalization)

If required, submit your response to your instructor for evaluation.

ANSWER KEY

I. Writing Activity: Support Strategies and Appeals
(Numerous possibilities exist for the revision of the sentences. What follows are possible revisions.)

Answer	Learning Objectives	Focus Points	References
1. B, D	LO 2, 3	FP 5, 6	video segment 3; textbook, pp. 282–285
2. B, C	LO 2, 3	FP 5, 6	video segment 3; textbook, pp. 282–285
3. A	LO 2, 3	FP 5, 6	video segment 3; textbook, pp. 282–285
4. A, B	LO 2, 3	FP 5, 6	video segment 3; textbook, pp. 282–285
5. B	LO 2, 3	FP 5, 6	video segment 3; textbook, pp. 282–285
6. A, B	LO 2, 3	FP 5, 6	video segment 3; textbook, pp. 282–285

II. Writing Activity: Counterargument
............LO 3............FP 7............video segment 5; textbook, pp. 286–287
(Your instructor will advise you about evaluating this assignment.)

III. Writing Activity: Revision
............LO 3............FP 12............video segment 6; textbook, pp. 298–300
(Your instructor will advise you about evaluating this assignment.)

IV. Writing Activity: Logical Fallacies
............LO 2............FP 9............video segment 3; textbook, pp. 289–291
(Your instructor will advise you about evaluating this assignment.)

Lesson 7

Responding to Arguments

There is no good in arguing with the inevitable. The only argument available with an east wind is to put on your overcoat.
—James Russell Lowell

THEME

How do you respond when your best friend disagrees with you? Do you give in? Do you argue your point of view? Do you see your friend's side of the argument in presenting your response? In this lesson, you will use these skills to respond to a formal argument, that of an individual, or a professor, or even a cultural argument. People, in general, also respond to arguments that are not stated directly in a text. People often respond to indirect arguments: movies, advertisements, billboards. In freshman composition courses, students most often respond to formal arguments (essay or editorial). They can respond to a particular text or person and to particular statements or claims. You might say, "How boring!"

Responding to an argument does not necessarily mean disagreement. The initial argument provides the position on a topic. You, the writer, have numerous options beyond agreement or disagreement. You might agree with the initial argument of the essay or the poem or the advertisement and extend the ideas with additional points, disagree with a particular point, redefine the issue, or point out some logical flaws. If you'll recall the argument with your best friend, be creative in your response. Disagree with your own objective comments about your own argument. Agree with certain parts of your friend's argument, but be prepared to present your response in a way that engages your best friend. You'll both be better arguers if you learn to respond objectively, critically, and in the spirit of your good friendship.

The truth is always the strongest argument.
—Sophocles

LESSON RESOURCES

Textbook: Mauk and Metz: *The Composition of Everyday Life*
- Chapter 7, "Responding to Arguments," pp. 302–357
- Chapter 15, "Rhetorical Handbook"
  - "Coherence and "Conciseness," pp.761–764
  - "Word Choice," pp. 775–777

Video: "Responding to Arguments" from the series *The Writer's Circle*

LESSON GOAL

You will communicate in writing the ability to understand the process of analyzing someone else's argument through application of the processes of invention, delivery, and revision.

LESSON LEARNING OBJECTIVES

1. Select a formal argument for a written response.
2. Determine why the response to the argument should make a difference to the audience.
3. Analyze the response to the formal argument using Toulmin's analytical tools.
4. Focus on voice and tone in developing a position for the formal argument.
5. Revise the response to the argument, paying particular attention to the voice and tone, based on feedback from peers.

LESSON FOCUS POINTS

1. Where does a writer find an argument that someone else has formulated?
2. What criteria should a writer use to determine which argument is appropriate for an argumentative response?
3. What are Toulmin's Analytical Tools? What is a claim? What are grounds? What is a warranting assumption?
4. How does the writer determine if the argument backs up the warranting assumption?
5. In evaluating an argument, why should a writer consider purpose?
6. Why is it important to know if the argument has public resonance?
7. How does a writer avoid character slams?
8. What is the invisible present "I"?
9. Why must a writer consider tone in responding to an argument?
10. Why is the thesis important in writing an argument of response?
11. How does a writer use support in responding to an argument?
12. What is the value of counterargument in responding to an argument?

13. What are some of the logical fallacies a writer should avoid in responding to an argument?
14. What are appropriate organizational strategies for a response to an argument?
15. When should a writer quote the original argument?
16. How does a writer integrate summary in a response to an argument?
17. How should a writer integrate paraphrase in a response to an argument?
18. How can a writer integrate Toulminian analysis, argument, and counterargument?

WRITERS INTERVIEWED

Macarena Hernandez, Editorial Columnist, *The Dallas Morning News,* Dallas TX
Richard Rodriguez, Essayist and Journalist, San Francisco, CA

SUGGESTED WRITING ASSIGNMENTS

Consult with your instructor and the course syllabus about requirements for any of the assignments listed below.

1. Write an essay based on a response to an argument, either agreeing with the argument and extending its points or disagreeing with a particular point, redefining the issue or pointing out logical flaws.
2. Choose an "in your face" essay (e.g., Michael Moore, Bill O'Reilly, etc.) and write a thesis, support, counterargument and concession that respond to the external argumentative essay. Use a tone or voice that clearly contrasts with the tone of the external argument.

> *I find you want me to furnish you with argument and intellect, too.*
> —Oliver Goldsmith

ENRICHMENT ACTIVITIES

Complete the following activities. An answer key and/or guidelines appear at the end of this lesson for each activity.

I. **Writing Activity: Applying Toulmin's Analytical Tools**
   For each of the three arguments below, respond to the argument by writing a responsive claim, grounds, and warranting assumption. Explain why each response is acceptable. If required, submit your response to your instructor for evaluation.

1. Freudian analysis is overused; therefore, new strategies for exploring patients' psychological makeup should be further developed.

2. The Association of College Administrators requires more state funding to serve freshman and sophomore students.

3. The Biology faculty at State University request that the University embark upon the proposed cloning program to allow the faculty more leeway to do essential research.

II. **Wrting Activity: Revising for Vitality, Coherence, and Conciseness**
   - Read pp. 754–764 in "The Rhetorical Handbook" in your textbook.
   - Revise the following passage from Jada's essay for style: elevated language, chatty language, unthoughtful language, wishy-washy language, pig-headed language, and formulaic language.
   - Revise for Sentence Vitality: active voice, wordiness, unnecessary expletives.
   - Finally, revise the passage for Coherence and Conciseness: purposeful writing, following the main point, accurate word choice, consistent verb tense, conventional punctuation, transitions, pronoun agreement, subject/verb agreement.
   - If required, submit your response to your instructor for evaluation.

   Right now, we have an all volunteer army. No draft. As a volunteer, I was sent to war for a year, but they kept me there another nine months, through a second rotation, because there were not enough replacements. And there were not enough replacements because there is no draft. Another problem with the "all volunteer" army is that almost none of the politician's kids are there. If the people who make decisions about the war don't have family over there, then nobody is really paying attention to the killed and wounded. Nobody is paying attention when there is not enough body armor, and the humvees are lacking armor. If some of their kids were there, and they were being wounded and dying, probably some of the problem would get fixed faster.

III. Writing Assignment: Attributives and Absolutes

Revise the excerpt below from an interview with Richard Rodriguez to attempt to work with absolutes and to clean up attributive phrases. Absolute phrases consist of a noun, modifiers, and a participle. Absolutes help intensify ideas to create more sophisticated, concise sentences. Absolute phrases add subtle variety to your essay helping you escape the march of subject/verb, subject/verb sentence patterns. An example of an absolute phrase would be, "The culprit hiding in the barn, the local sheriff knocked at the ranch house door."

Attributive phrases connect a writer and his or her ideas. Be cautious of clumsy phrasing when you make those connections. Be aware of not drawing attention to the act of writing or to the author's thoughts. Boil the sentences down. For example, "In *The Grapes of Wrath* by John Steinbeck, Steinbeck writes about the poverty of the tenant farmers in the Dust Bowl in Oklahoma." Boil down the sentence to say, "In *The Grapes of Wrath,* John Steinbeck writes about the poverty of the tenant farmers in the Dust Bowl in Oklahoma.

If required, submit your revision to your instructor for evaluation.

Who says Shakespeare is such a great writer? If you want to write an essay about why Shakespeare is not a great writer, you may write that essay. You may say that in your first sentence: I think Shakespeare is an overrated writer. But realize that by the time you have finished that sentence about Shakespeare, by the time I have finished reading your sentence, I have come with all my defenses. I have come to feel, "Who is this idiot? What does she know about Shakespeare who wrote comedies and tragedies and the weaknesses of man? Has she read everything by Shakespeare? Does she understand any of his plays? Has she really understood Shakespeare's plays?" In other words, you really have to prove your arrogance and your knowledge of Shakespeare.

                         Richard Rodriguez

ANSWER KEY

| Answer | Learning Objectives | Focus Points | References |

I. Writing Activity: Applying Toulmin's Analytical Tools
............LO 3 ....FP 3, 4..........................video segment 3; textbook, pp. 340–343
(Your instructor will advise you about evaluating this assignment.)

II. Writing Activity: Revising for Vitality, Coherence, and Conciseness
............LO 5 ....FP 9, 14.........................video segment 5; textbook, pp. 754–764
(Your instructor will advise you about evaluating this assignment.)

III. Writing Activity: Attributives and Absolutes
............LO 4, 5 ....FP 9, 14...textbook, p. 355
(Your instructor will advise you about evaluating this assignment.)

Lesson 8

Evaluating and Organizing

For every problem, there is one solution which is simple, neat and wrong.
—Henry Louis Mencken

THEME

Evaluation plays a role in everyday life as well as in your college classes. We all evaluate the morning news on television, or the neighbor's new automobile, or the qualities of the figures on a billboard. In this lesson you will evaluate a topic based on specific, reasonable criteria to make a choice about the best option available to you.

Evaluating is the act of judging the value or worth of a given subject. A formal process is necessary for sound evaluation whether you are selecting a course to attend, an apartment to rent, or an appetizer in a restaurant. The ability to make formal evaluations is essential to academic thinking and writing. In the fields of biology, law enforcement, crime scene investigation, civil engineering, English, and art, formal evaluation is essential.

The student who can evaluate well and make judgments outside of personal tastes is able to make valuable, carefully thought-out decisions. Those decisions help distinguish the best course of action and clarify options when many seem available.

LESSON RESOURCES

Textbook: Mauk and Metz: *The Composition of Everyday Life*
- Chapter 8, "Evaluating," pp. 358–405
- Chapter 15, "Rhetorical Handbook"
  - "Writing Style," pp. 754–760

Video: "Evaluating and Organizing" from the series *The Writer's Circle*

Freedom from the desire for an answer is essential to the understanding of a problem.
—J. Krishnamurti

LESSON GOAL

You will communicate the ability to make judgments outside of personal tastes in making valuable decisions, distinguishing the best course of action and clarifying options when many seem available.

LESSON LEARNING OBJECTIVES

1. Develop criteria for evaluating processes in a formal evaluation of a subject in the major field or a literary work for an argumentative evaluation essay.
2. Make judgments outside of personal tastes to make a decision, to distinguish the best course of action, and to clarify options in developing a formal argumentative evaluation.
3. Incorporate the elements of evaluation to develop a formal argument.
4. Revise the formal argumentative evaluation to avoid wordiness and repetition and to add missing information where needed.

LESSON FOCUS POINTS

1. How may a writer discover and apply criteria to a subject? What are appropriate criteria for a subject of evaluation?
2. How may a writer best develop an evaluative argument?
3. What is important to include in a thesis for an evaluative argument?
4. How does a writer use the elements of evaluation in an evaluative argument?
5. Why is the presentation of the subject important in an evaluative argument?
6. How do analysis and application of criteria determine the outcomes in an evaluative argument?
7. Why are the elements of argument, support, counterargument, concessions, evidence, and appeals necessary to an argument of evaluation?
8. How does the writer support the claims of the argument in an evaluation? How does support outside the subject allow the writer to further the argument of evaluation?
9. How should a writer arrange the elements of evaluation in an argument? When should the writer change paragraphs in an argument of evaluation?
10. How may a writer avoid harsh description in an essay of evaluation? Avoid the enthusiasm crisis? Include asides?
11. How is intensive description instrumental in an argumentative essay of evaluation? How can allusion assist a writer of an essay of evaluation?
12. What are global revision strategies? In what ways are writers able to use these strategies?

Lesson 8—Evaluating and Organizing

WRITERS INTERVIEWED

Jenny Anmuth, Travel Editor and Writer, Frommer's Travel Guides, South Salem, NY
Matt Zoller Seitz, Film and Television Critic, *New York Press/Newark Star Ledger,* Brooklyn, NY

SUGGESTED WRITING ASSIGNMENTS

Consult with your instructor and the course syllabus about requirements for any of the assignments listed below.

1. Write a formal evaluation essay on a subject related to your major by using various approaches and making judgments outside of personal tastes.
2. Examine Stayer's essay, "Whales R Us," pp. 366-371 in your text and Whitehead's essay, "Rethinking Divorce," pp. 379-381 in your text. In a paragraph for each essay, describe their voices and point to particular passages that best illustrate your description. Discuss the value and liability of both strategies.
3. Find an image that you think goes with one of the essays in Chapter 8, "Evaluating," and explain in writing what you think the relationship is between the image and the essay. How might the image help to illustrate a point being made in the essay? Or how might it encourage the reader to think about a certain point?
4. Explain how someone might view the image differently after having read the appropriate essay. Be specific in explaining how the person might view the image before reading the essay and after reading the essay.
5. In a short essay, reflect upon an evaluation expressed in writing or otherwise that has influenced many people. For example, people (such as government officials, college administrators, drivers of motor vehicles, etc.) often make evaluations that impact others. Whom did they affect and how?

Eureka! I have found it.

—Archimedes

Lesson 8—Evaluating and Organizing

ENRICHMENT ACTIVITIES

Complete the following activities. An answer key and/or guidelines appear at the end of this lesson for each activity.

I. Writing Activity: Vitality
Vitality in writing involves writing sharp, intense sentences. To develop sentence vitality, do the following:
- Avoid Unnecessary Interruption: move interrupting elements which disrupt sentence flow to keep the main parts of the sentence together.
- Repeat Clause or Phrase Patterns: repetition can add vitality and intensity. Repetitions create familiar linguistic territory and drive points home.
- Condense Wordy Phrases: clean out the excess words.

In the first two paragraphs of Marcus' essay (See Writing Activity II below), rewrite for vitality. Pay particular attention to unnecessary interruption and excess wordiness and condense or revise those phrases. If required, submit to your revision to your instructor for evaluation.

II. Writing Activity: Analysis of an Essay
Answer the following questions about Marcus' essay to explain how he used criteria (or did not use criteria).
- What does the film *Raging Bull* try to achieve according to the essay? Be specific.
- What is the audience of the essay and of the subject of the essay, the movie *Raging Bull*? Imagine who might use, benefit from, and interact with *Raging Bull*?
- What goals should the film *Raging Bull* and other films like it have?
- Does the essay evaluate the film adequately?
- What are the criteria that Marcus used to measure the film? Was he successful? What criteria did he leave out, if any?
- If required, submit your analysis to your instructor for evaluation.

Draft of Marcus' Essay

By anyone's standards, Martin Scorcese's *Raging Bull* ranks as one of the masterpieces of contemporary cinema. In a 1989 poll of major film critics, this knockout screen story of real-life boxing champ Jake La Morra was voted the best movie of the decade. Its stunning black and white cinematography, visceral editing, and groundbreaking sound design showcase an unforgettable performance by the great American actor, Robert DeNiro. The Special Collector's Edition DVD, presenting the film in its original widescreen version along with many extra features, is well worth the investment.

Many DVDs feature a commentary track from the director, but the Collector's Edition goes above and beyond. With three separate commentary tracks and four documentaries on the making of the film, its examination of the film is exhaustive. The documentaries give a decent overview of the script to screen process, but for the film lover, the real rewards are in the commentary tracks. The first is from director Martin Scorcese and his longtime editor Thelma Schoonmaker. The second provides insights from the producers, the cinematographer, the music producer, and the supervising sound editor. Yet a third track features the three screenwriters and Jake La Motta himself, who consulted on the picture.

People think of the film director as the leading auteur, but this wealth of commentaries makes it clear how much collaboration goes into the making of a masterpiece. Take, for example, the opening credits. The image of DeNiro as La Motta, in a leopard skin robe, bouncing and shadow boxing gracefully around the ring, highlighted by intermittently popping flashbulbs, remains one of the film's most memorable sequences. We learn from the commentary that the flashes, which became a visual trademark of the movie, were created by cinematographer Michael Chapman, employing vintage 1940s flash bulbs that produce a slow, dramatic decay of light. The theme music for the sequence was chosen by Scorcese, but it was music producer Robbie Robertson who had the idea to put it through a reverb processor, then strip away the main track and use just the echo. The result is a haunting, interior quality that sets the tone for the entire film. When married to the slow motion images, it seems as though the music is coming from inside La Motta himself. Interestingly, learning about these extensive collaborations doesn't diminish our regard for Scorcese, but rather points out how a masterful director is constantly integrating the contributions of many other remarkable talents.

Boxing fans and diehard Scorcese freaks may rush out to buy this comprehensive archive, but why should the rest of us spend twenty dollars of our hard earned money to own it? The main reason is that it makes this classic American film more accessible and enjoyable. Not everyone can relate to Jake La Motta's violent and self-destructive life, but getting inside the cinematic process leads us to a deeper appreciation of the film, and of filmmaking in general. This level of work deserves to be understood and celebrated. It elevates us all.

III. Writing Activity: Developing and Applying Criteria

When you develop criteria on a subject, you must understand what a subject is trying to achieve for a particular audience. To develop criteria, ask yourself the following questions:
- What does the subject try to achieve?
- What do other subjects try to achieve?
- What is the subject's audience?
- What goals should this subject, or all subjects like it, have?

For example, you might be discussing a local fast food restaurant. Skippy's is trying to achieve low cost, quick service, and tasty food. Those three items could make up the criteria you're using to evaluate a variety of fast food restaurants. Which has the lowest cost, quickest service, and tastiest food?

To apply criteria to a subject answer the following questions:
- In what particular ways does the subject achieve its goal? What specific parts, tools, or strategies help the subject to achieve its goal?
- In what particular ways does the subject fall short of achieving its goal?
- What goals does the subject ignore?
- How does the subject compare to and contrast with other similar subjects?
- What is unique about your subject's approach or strategy to achieving its goal?

In the exercise that follows, circle appropriate criteria for evaluating an item in each category. Then, select which three criteria would best fit the scenario that follows each item. Check the answer key for possible responses.

1. Luxury Hotels
    A. Location
    B. Amenities
    C. Cost
    D. Beauty queens
    E. Restaurant facilities
    F. Room service

Marcus is planning to spend the night at the Atlantis Hotel in the Bahamas. He has a budget, but he can afford to be a little extravagant. He is meeting a friend there and wants to impress her with a romantic evening, dinner, and dancing under the stars. Marcus is into fitness, so he wants to take advantage of the spa and the gym on site. List three criteria from above that apply to his romantic vacation.

_____
_____
_____

Lesson 8—Evaluating and Organizing

2. Automobiles
    A. Color
    B. New or used
    C. Passenger capability (size)
    D. Engine specifications
    E. Status symbol
    F. Model

Jada plans to buy a new car, one that will get her where she wants to go. She doesn't care what age the car is, but she does care about the color. Jada wants a red car that can carry her and at least three of her girlfriends to their social activities. She knows nothing about the mechanical workings of cars, but she does want a car that will start when she turns the key in the ignition. List three criteria from the list above that apply to her purchase of a car.

_____
_____
_____

3. Colleges
    A. Distance from home
    B. Degrees offered
    C. Accreditation
    D. Number of programs
    E. Size
    F. Good looking guys

Rosa is planning to transfer to a four-year university, and she is concerned about being too far away from her husband and children. She is looking for a good pre-law institution with renowned professors and good standing in the legal world. She doesn't really care if the university has many students. She is just concerned about the pre-law program. List the three criteria above that apply to her choice of a university.

_____
_____
_____

Lesson 8—Evaluating and Organizing

4. Movies
   A. Entertainment value
   B. Rating
   C. Good popcorn
   D. Stars
   E. Budget
   F. Comfort of theater

   Lakshmi wants to take her children to a first run movie at the local theater. Since she is the family breadwinner, she pays attention to the costs of three tickets, so she chooses a matinee. She believes her children will enjoy the movie which was advertised as an educational and entertaining film on a local children's cable channel. Two unknown actors play the major roles in the film, but Lakshmi doesn't really care about the actors. Lakshmi's concern is with the educational value for her children. List the three criteria that apply to her choice of a movie.

   _____
   _____
   _____

IV. **Writing Activity: Voice**
   Review the draft of Marcus' essay in Writing Activity II and pay attention to his voice. Rewrite passages that reflect harsh description, too much enthusiasm, breaking boundaries, asides, and intensive description. The strategies are listed below:
   - Avoiding Harsh Description: avoid harsh words like "ridiculous" or "dumb" to keep from revealing your own aggression. Don't distract readers from the subject, but prompt the reader to investigate the subject more closely.
   - Avoiding the Enthusiasm Crisis: try not to overwhelm your reader with enthusiasm. Too much enthusiasm alienates your reader.
   - Exploring the Boundaries: stay in your comfort zone, the place you feel most at ease. However, the most comfortable voice may not be the most appropriate for the situation. Work with various voices, depending on the writing situation.
   - Asides: Writers use parentheses or dashes to make an aside or ask a rhetorical question, often on a more personal note than the voice of the essay. It's a way for the writer to directly address the reader and engage the reader.
   - Intensive Description: Voices often hide behind abstraction. Your voice becomes more obvious when you use particular and focused words. Use characterizations that do more than describe. Create a presence in your writing.

Select at least three of the strategies above to revise short passages from Marcus' essay (See Enrichment Activity 2 above). If required, submit your revisions to your instructor for evaluation.

ANSWER KEY

| | Learning | Focus | |
|Answer | Objectives | Points | References |

I. Writing Exercise: Vitality
................LO 4 ....FP 12 ....video segment 6; textbook, pp. 402–403
(Your instructor will advise you about evaluating this assignment.)

II. Writing Activity: Analysis of an Essay
................LO 1 ....FP 1, 2, 4, 6, 8................................ video segments 3, 4; textbook, pp. 386–387
(Your instructor will advise you about evaluating this assignment.)

III. Writing Activity: Developing and Applying Criteria
(Numerous possibilities exist for the choices of criteria for each item. What follows are possible choices.)
1. A, B, E ..... LO 1 ....FP 1, 6 .... video segments 1, 2; textbook, pp. 384–387
2. A, B, C ..... LO 1 ....FP 1, 6 .... video segments 1, 2; textbook, pp. 384–387
3. A, B, C ..... LO 1 ....FP 1, 6 .... video segments 1, 2; textbook, pp. 384–387
4. A, B, E ..... LO 1 ....FP 1, 6 .... video segments 1, 2; textbook, pp. 384–387

IV. Writing Activity: Voice
................LO 4 ....FP 10, 11 ....video segment 6; textbook, pp. 400–401
(Your instructor will advise you about evaluating this assignment.)

Lesson 9

Integrating Research

Basic research is what I'm doing when I don't know what I'm doing.
—Werner Von Braun

THEME

In this lesson, you will learn the skills necessary to find information, reflect upon that information, and present that information in a formal research paper. Many students look upon the term "research paper" with dread. But, actually, doing research and finding information are enjoyable activities. You will learn to locate sources from books, journal articles, newspapers, search engines, databases, and the Internet. Not only will you learn to find information, but you will also learn the skills to document that information appropriately within your paper and in a list of sources. You don't want to be accused of plagiarism, do you? That's why you must document the information from every external source you examine in your research.

The most important thing to remember about doing research is to involve yourself in a process. Determine your topic. What are you interested in learning more about either in your major or for your own enlightenment? Pose that as a narrow question. Don't research AIDS, but do more specific refinement. AIDS in African children is a narrower topic, and a narrow topic lends itself to more specific research.

Next, begin to locate the information on your topic in a variety of places, not just the Internet. The Internet may be a valuable source for information, but often, unreliable information appears on the Internet. So expand your horizons, find books, journal articles, news stories, information from databases, interviews with experts, and surveys that support your topic. Once you have your information, organize it and write a brilliant research paper. It's simple: just follow a process!

Errors using inadequate data are much less than those using no data at all.
—Charles Babbage

LESSON RESOURCES

Textbook: Mauk and Metz: *The Composition of Everyday Life*
- Chapter 13, "Research and Writing: Gathering and Using Information from Sources," pp. 610–697

Video: "Integrating Research" from the series *The Writer's Circle*

LESSON GOAL

As you apply the processes of invention, delivery and revision to a researched argument, you will communicate the ability to apply the standard rules of research for the format of a research document which integrates the ideas of others as well as your own ideas.

LESSON LEARNING OBJECTIVES

1. Apply basic research methods in gathering and organizing information from a variety of sources for a researched argument.
2. Quote, paraphrase, and summarize information gathered from external sources in a researched argument.
3. Integrate external source information with your own opinion on the topic.
4. Avoid plagiarism in argumentative research.
5. Revise the argumentative research to insure that sources are adequately integrated and properly cited.

LESSON FOCUS POINTS

1. What are issues to consider and discuss when writing a research paper?
2. Why should a writer seek information from external sources? When should a writer seek information from external sources? Where are the best places to find information?
3. What is plagiarism? Why should a writer avoid plagiarism?
4. Why should a writer document sources? What is the difference between formal and informal documentation?
5. What is primary research? What is observation?
6. How does a writer conduct an interview for external information? What are the best questions? Why should the interview and interview questions be planned? How is the interview used in the text of the research?
7. What are surveys? How does the writer determine the best questions for a survey? Whom should the writer survey?
8. How does a writer use survey responses in the text of the research?
9. What is secondary research? How is the library a source of secondary research? How is the Internet a source of secondary research?
10. How should a writer evaluate external sources? What are the best ways to evaluate Internet resources?
11. What is paraphrase? What is summary? How are note cards useful in research?
12. How does a writer integrate quotations into the text of the research? What are the best ways to integrate sources in the research? How should quotations be punctuated?
13. What is MLA style? What is APA style? How do MLA and APA differ?

WRITERS INTERVIEWED

Carol Berkin, Historian and Author, Baruch College, CUNY, New York, NY
Laeta Kalogridis, Screenwriter, Encino, CA

SUGGESTED WRITING ASSIGNMENT

Consult with your instructor and the course syllabus about requirements for the assignment listed below.

Write an argumentative research paper by integrating external sources with your own opinion on the topic through paraphrase, summary, or quote.

If we knew what we were doing, it wouldn't be called research, would it?
—Albert Einstein

ENRICHMENT ACTIVITIES

Complete the following activities. An answer key and/or guidelines appear at the end of this lesson for each activity.

I. Writing Exercise: Punctuating Quotations
Review your textbook "Punctuating Quotations," pp. 644–648. Rewrite the quoted information in the exercise that follows, using appropriate punctuation. Check the answer key at the end of this lesson for possible responses.

Tell whether each item in numbered paragraphs below is one of the following:
- Quotation marks only
- Speaking verb followed by a comma
  - Quotation at the beginning of a sentence
  - Quotation in the middle of a sentence
  - Quotation at the end of a sentence
  - Quotation divided by your own words
- Sentence followed by a colon
  - Quote connected with a colon
  - Quote connected with a cue or transitional expression
- Omitting words
- Adding words
- Noting an error
- Using lengthy quotes
- Double quotes

1. As John Steinbeck states in The Chrysanthemums On every side it sat like a lid on the mountains and made of the great valley a closed pot.

2. Dark had descended on the brilliancy of the March afternoon, and the grinding rasping street life of the city was at its highest begins Edith Wharton in her story, Pomegranate Seed.

3. (Note to student: Add words or notes or comments within the quote in this passage.) I was popular in certain circles, says Aunt Rose. I wasn't no thinner then, only more stationary in the flesh. In time to come, Lillie, don't be surprised---change is a fact of God. From this no one is excused. (Grace Paley)

4. D.H. Lawrence writes in The Horse Dealer's Daughter, Almost immediately, he heard her coming down. She had on her best dress of black voile, and her hair was tidy, but still damp. She looked at him---and in spite of herself, smiled. I don't like you in those clothes she said. Do I look a sight? He answered. They were shy of one another. I'll make you some tea she said. No, I must go.

5. Raising his eyebrow, Professor Jones requests that it behooves you to turn your work in at the appropriate time.

6. (Note to student: Note the errors in the passage that are grammatically or syntactically flawed. Use square brackets and the three letter word *sic* directly after the error.) Only a person like your mama stands on one foot, she don't notice how big her behind is getting and sings in the canary's ear for thirty years. Who's listening? Pap's in the shop. You and Seymour, thinking about yourself. So she waits in a spotless kitchen for a kind word and thinks---poor Rosie... (Grace Paley)

7. (Note to student: Use an ellipsis in this passage by omitting a sentence and inserting the appropriate punctuation.) Vaughn's not there the next Saturday and the Saturday after that and the third Saturday he's not there I begin thinking that I'm thinking more about him than I do of anybody or thing and spending more time looking at the staircase and around the platform for him that I do for those young men. I've gradually lost interest in finding them and over the last four months my chances have gotten worse and worse that I'll even recognize them. If they ever do come down here and as far as their repeating that harassing-the-girl incident at this particular station, well forget it, and I leave the station at noon instead of around my usual two and decide that was my last Saturday there.

Stephen Dixon

8. Stephen Crane noted in The Blue Hotel We, five of us, have collaborated in the murder of this Swede.

II. Writing Activity: Role of Research
Respond to the questions below regarding the role of your research topic in everyday life. If required, submit your responses to your instructor for discussion and evaluation.

1. When and why do you refer to sources on your topic in everyday life?

2. How might sources contribute to a writer's credibility?

3. Why should information gained from a source be documented?

4. When is informal documentation acceptable?

5. How can a researcher like you evaluate the reliability of information from a source?

6. Why do you get information from a source on your topic?

7. When do you get information from a source on your topic?

8. What is inventive research?

9. Where do you get information from sources on your topic?

10. What is plagiarism? How do you avoid plagiarizing?

Lesson 9—Integrating Research

11. Why should you document sources on your topic?

    _____
    _____
    _____

12. Why is your topic a good research topic?

    _____
    _____
    _____

13. What is the difference in formal and informal documentation?

    _____
    _____
    _____

III. Writing Activity: Summarizing and Paraphrasing

Rewrite four of the passages below as a summary or as a paraphrase. Write at least two summaries and at least two paraphrases. If required, submit them to your instructor for evaluation.

1. Remember that paraphrases avoid using the same subjects and verbs as the original text. A paraphrase is a rewording of the original source using your own words and expressions. A paraphrase conveys the detail and complexity of the original text.

2. Remember that summary involves expressing ideas from a source in your own words instead of the words of the source. Summary removes much of the detail while still dealing with the complexity of the ideas.

    A. A photographer told me about a talented and highly skilled artisan who touched up photographs. He was the best in our region of the country, and people knew it; because the demand for his skill was so great, he was unable to keep up with the work. A few years ago, however, this artisan suddenly closed his shop; he did not have enough work to stay in business. Due to developments in computer hardware and software, anyone with just a little training can now achieve results previously attainable by only a few highly skilled artisans. Technology has rendered this artisan's skills obsolete. And this is not an isolated case; technology is antiquating many skills.

    "Why a Great Books Education is the Most Practical"   David Crabtree, Ph.D.

B. Computers can undoubtedly contribute wonders to the field of education. In fact, computer education is a must if children intend to thrive in modern society. The possibilities are endless when it comes to surfing the Web or using the thousands of educational programs currently available. These programs are capable of reading text on a computer with icons beside words that take students to a galaxy of options, icons to learn more about the era in which the text was written, fascinating facts about the author, and helpful notes about the morals of the story. But computers are being used more and more frequently as a substitute for books, blackboards, and in some cases, the teachers themselves.

"Floppy Disk Fallacies" — Elizabeth Bohnhorst

C. According to the United Nations International Narcotics Control Board (INCB), advanced countries are overdosing on quick-fix pills to ease "non-medical" problems like fat and stress. INCB also stated that mood-altering drugs are often prescribed for social problems, such as unemployment or relationship problems. Consumers around the globe are taking medication for this disease called life. The fact that people are spending their hard-earned money on medicine they do not need is bad enough, but the harm these unnecessary drugs can do is a much bigger issue. Yet the drug companies keep on telling us, "It's okay, just ask your doctor." The problem is, the doctors don't have all the answers, either.

"Beware of Drug Sales" — Therese Cherry

D. Advertisers spend an enormous amount of money on psychological research. As the chairman of one advertising agency says, "If you want to get into people's wallets, first you have to get into their lives." As a result, they understand addiction very well. Soon after I began my study of alcohol advertising, I realized with horror that alcohol advertisers understand alcoholism perhaps better than any other group in the country. And they use this knowledge to keep people in denial.

"Addiction as a Relationship" — Jean Kilbourne

E. A look at the evolution of the comic strip shows how the "funnies," in their own way, record history. The "Yellow Kid," born in 1895 in the New York World, is generally accepted as the first comic character. A violent, gangster-talking figure, the Kid would probably be banned from today's papers. His comments and struggles, however, echoed reality for the city's slum dwellers. Though the Kid died, comics, with their solid psychological appeal, were here to stay.

"Cartoons 'n Comics: Communication to the Quick" — Joy Clough

F. In the mainstream perspective, humans are either driven by media images or they are entirely independent thinkers. They either see something and buy a car or they decide not to buy a car. They either want a certain pair of blue jeans or they don't even imagine themselves wanting them. Such a perspective ignores the complexities of desire and the power of images. Of course, people do not simply run to the car lot and buy an SUV after seeing an ad in Time. But they consume the image and the apparent value of the image. When we see an image (whether it be a hairdo, a body type, or a vehicle), we also get an assumption about its worth in the culture. And this assumption stays with us. It molds into our sense of daily life. (This is, of course, why corporations spend millions of dollars to place images everywhere---so that our ideas about daily life naturally come to include the product or the image.

"The Mighty Image"   Cameron Johnson

IV. Writing Activity: Plagiarism

1. Find an article on the Internet or in a magazine or professional journal or newspaper on the topic of plagiarism and its related issues. The article might be about plagiarism software or high profilers accused of plagiarism, or what instructors are doing about plagiarism in higher education. Find an article and summarize the content. Relate it to your own experience. If required, submit your findings to your instructor.

ANSWER KEY

I. Writing Activity: Punctuating Quotations
(Numerous possibilities exist for the revision of the sentences. What follows are possible revisions.)

Answer	Learning Objectives	Focus Points	References

1. ....LO 2 ....FP 12..video segment 3; textbook, pp. 644–648
   As John Steinbeck states in "The Chrysanthemums," "On every side it sat like a lid on the mountains and made of the great valley a closed pot."
   - Speaking verb followed by a comma; quotation at the end of a sentence

2. ....LO 1 ....FP 12..video segment 3; textbook, pp. 644–648
   "Dark had descended on the brilliancy of the March afternoon, and the grinding rasping street life of the city was at its highest," begins Edith Wharton in her story, "Pomegranate Seed."
   - Quotation marks only

3. ....LO 1 ....FP 12..video segment 3; textbook, pp. 644–648
   "'I was popular in certain circles,' says Aunt Rose. 'I wasn't no thinner then, only more stationary in the flesh. In time to come, Lillie, [her sister] don't be surprised…change is a fact of God. From this no one is excused.'"
   - Adding words; double quotes

4. ....LO 1 ....FP 12..video segment 3; textbook, pp. 644–648
   D.H. Lawrence writes in "The Horse Dealer's Daughter," "Almost immediately, he heard her coming down. She had on her best dress of black voile, and her hair was tidy but still damp. She looked at him… and in spite of herself, smiled."
   'I don't like you in those clothes,' she said.
   'Do I look a sight?' he answered.
   They were shy of one another.
   'I'll make you some tea,' she said.
   'No, I must go.'"
   - Speaking verb followed by a quote in mid-sentence; double quotes

5. ....LO 1 ....FP 12.. video segment 3; textbook, pp. 644-648
   Raising his eyebrow, Professor Jones requests that "it behooves you to turn your work in at the appropriate time."
   - Quote connected with a cue or transitional expression

6. ....LO 1 ....FP 12.. video segment 3; textbook, pp. 644-648
   "Only a person like your mama stands on one foot, [sic] she don't [sic] notice how big her behind is getting and sings in the canary's ear for thirty years. Who's listening? Pap's in the shop. You and Seymour, thinking about yourself. [sic] So she waits in a spotless kitchen for a kind word and thinks…'poor Rosie'."
   - Noting an error

7. ....LO 1 ....FP 12.. video segment 3; textbook, pp. 644-648
   "Vaughn's not there the next Saturday and the Saturday after that and the third Saturday he's not there I begin thinking that I'm thinking more about him than I do of anybody or thing and spending more time looking at the staircase and around the platform for him that I do for those young men….If they ever do come down here and as far as their repeating that harassing-the-girl incident at this particular station, well forget it, and I leave the station at noon instead of around my usual two and decide that was my last Saturday there."
   - Omitting words

	Learning	Focus	
Answer	Objectives	Points	References

8. ....LO 1...................FP 12.. video segment 3; textbook, pp. 644-648
Stephen Crane noted in "The Blue Hotel": "We, five of us, have collaborated in the murder of this Swede."
- Sentence followed by a colon; quote connected with a colon

II. Writing Activity: Role of Research
...............LO 1, 3...............FP 1–13................................ video segments 1, 2, 3; textbook, pp. 612–697
(Your instructor will advise you about evaluating this assignment.)

III. Writing Activity: Summarizing and Paraphrasing
..................LO 2.....................FP 11..video segment 3; textbook, pp. 638–640
(Your instructor will advise you about evaluating this assignment.)

IV. Writing Activity: Plagiarism
...................LO 4...................FP 3...................... video segment 3; textbook, p. 613 and p. 639
(Your instructor will advise you about evaluating this assignment.)

Lesson 10

Searching for Causes

Cause and effect, means and ends, seed and fruit cannot be severed; for the effect already blooms in the cause, the end preexists in the means, the fruit in the seed.

—Ralph Waldo Emerson

THEME

How much time do we all spend trying to figure out the "whys" of events or behaviors or trends in our everyday lives? Often, we discover not just one but several "whys" or causes to our wonderings. Why did she react to my question so passionately? Why is it that Professor Unger will not understand that we all have other things going on in our lives, like work and social activities?

College courses constantly present students with possibilities and causes. Discovering causes is the issue in most academic inquiries. We explore, ruminate, uncover, discover, and dig until we find the myriad answers and decide on the most appropriate cause of the topic at hand. This lesson will assist you in your search for causes. You will hone your research and evaluative skills by interviewing others and doing external research. As you draft your argument, you will learn ways to create credibility, project wonder, and avoid preachiness. In your search, ferret out the hidden causes of the "whys" you are investigating and report them accurately and fully to your chosen audience.

The task of the real intellectual consists of analyzing illusions in order to discover their causes.

—Arthur Miller

LESSON RESOURCES

Textbook: Mauk and Metz: *The Composition of Everyday Life*
- Chapter 9, "Searching for Causes," pp. 406–451
- Chapter 15, "Rhetorical Handbook"
  - "Opening and Closing Paragraphs," pp. 752–753
  - "Phrases," p. 802

Video: "Searching for Causes" from the series *The Writer's Circle*

LESSON GOAL

You will communicate an attempt to find the answers in a search for causes of behaviors, events and trends in everyday life by practicing the processes of invention, delivery, and revision.

LESSON LEARNING OBJECTIVES

1. Research questions that lead to developing critical perspectives on behaviors, events, and trends.
2. Research a possible cause for a behavior, event or trend after focusing on a particular topic.
3. Develop an argument in favor of a particular cause using surveys and external research.
4. Attempt various support strategies to increase the credibility of the writer's voice in writing a causal argument.
5. Revise the causal argument after participating in a peer review session.

LESSON FOCUS POINTS

1. How does a writer find a topic about the cause of some event, behavior, or trend?
2. How does the writer determine the cause? How will outside sources assist the writer in finding the cause? How will surveys assist the writer in determining cause?
3. Why does the topic matter to others?
4. Why is the thesis integral to an argumentative essay of cause?
5. How does a writer develop support for an argumentative essay of cause?
6. What is counterargument? How is counterargument useful in an argumentative essay of cause?
7. What are concessions? How are concessions useful in an argumentative essay of cause?
8. Where should the subject and its causes be explained in the essay?
9. What about other causes? Where do they fit in the essay?
10. How should the writer integrate outside sources? How should the writer use paragraphs?
11. How does a writer create credibility in an argumentative essay of cause?
12. How does a writer project wonder in an argumentative essay of cause?
13. How does a writer avoid preachiness in an argumentative essay of cause?
14. What are the best revision strategies for a writer to use in a final draft of an argumentative essay of cause?

WRITERS INTERVIEWED

Carol Berkin, Historian and Author, Baruch College, City University of New York, New York, NY

Richard Rodriguez, Essayist and Journalist, San Francisco, CA

John Philip Santos, Author and Poet, San Antonio, TX

SUGGESTED WRITING ASSIGNMENTS

Consult with your instructor and the course syllabus about requirements for any of the assignments listed below.

1. Write an argument essay of cause with the purpose of finding the answers in a search for causes of behaviors, events, or trends in everyday life.
2. Write a letter to your instructor explaining why the main idea of your essay of cause is significant. Your letter should touch on the essay's public resonance and how it might affect a reader's thinking or behavior.
3. Find an image that relates to your essay of cause and write a caption for the image. Then, write an explanation of the relationship between your image and your text. Next, show the image to several people and ask each person to read your essay. Then, ask them how they view the image you chose differently after they have read your essay.

Every cause produces more than one effect.
—Herbert Spencer

ENRICHMENT ACTIVITIES

Complete the following activities. An answer key and/or guidelines appear at the end of this lesson for each activity.

I. Writing Activity: Invention
Look at the "Point of Contact" section of your text on p. 432. Research and write your personal responses to the questions on one of the topics on the page: work, local events, social trends, campus issues, politics, and your major. Write a summary of your findings. If required, submit your summary to your instructor.

II. Writing Activity: Opening and Closing Paragraphs
Read the following opening and closing paragraphs from a draft of Richard's essay in Lesson Ten of the course video. Review the guidelines below to determine if the introduction and conclusion are appropriate.

1. Rewrite the introduction to Richard's draft following the guidelines in the bulleted list below. In your revision, use at least three guidelines from the list. Include comments about the process you followed in your revision.

   Strategies for Introductions:
   - Begin with a statistic, quotation, or anecdote.
   - Ask a question.
   - Create a strong visual image.
   - Provide necessary background.
   - Make a comparison.
   - Briefly explain what the essay is responding to.
   - Allude to the public resonance of the essay.
   - Create a tone for the essay.

   Richard's introduction:
   Being from Texas, I have always known that I came from a long line of Texans. We consider Texan to be closer to a nationality than the designation of a mere state. We think of ourselves as mavericks, frontier people. Our ancestors abandoned the old South and came west with their wagons and their families and their guns to make a new South. They left behind the frilly clothes and fancy affectations of a dying culture for the promise of a new life. What they didn't leave behind was their slaves.

2. Rewrite the conclusion to Richard's draft following the guidelines in the bulleted list below. In your revision, use at least three guidelines from the list. Include comments about the process you followed in your revision.

   Strategies for Conclusions:
   - Suggest or emphasize the public resonance.
   - State and explain the main idea.
   - Create a strong image.
   - Ask an important question.
   - Relate back to a point from the introduction.
   - Call the reader to thought or action.
   - Make a recommendation.
   - Suggest a consequence.

   Richard's conclusion:
   For a state that thinks of itself as first in all things, when it comes to slavery Texas always seems to come in last. It was the last slave state admitted to the union. It was also the last state to emancipate its slaves, waiting until June 19, 1865, a full two months after Lee's surrender to Grant at Appomattox, before delivering its emancipation proclamation. Now maybe that was due to the slow lines of communication back in those days, and maybe it wasn't. But what I want to know is, why are we

also the last to acknowledge our slave-owning history? Do we actually believe our own hype so completely that we've forgotten who and where we really came from?

If required, submit both paragraphs with your comments about the process you followed to your instructor.

III. Writing Activity: Voice (Preachiness and Projecting Wonder)

1. Review the essay in your text by Susan Jacoby, "When Bright Girls Decide That Math Is a 'Waste of Time'" (pp. 426–427). Identify two or three sentences that provide examples of "preachiness" (writing that demeans people or tells people what they need). Rewrite those sentences to avoid preachiness. If required, submit both the examples from the textbook and your revisions to your instructor.

2. Review the essay in your text by Leonard Kress, "Throwing Up Childhood" (pp. 416–420). Identify two or three sentences that should project wonder but do not. Projecting wonder creates a sense of curiosity, even wonder. "I wonder if…." Rewrite those sentences to project wonder. If required, submit both examples from your textbook and your revisions to your instructor.

IV. Writing Activity: Strings of Phrases

Writers sometimes string together several prepositional phrases. (A prepositional phrase begins with a preposition such as in, of, between, on, beside, behind, for, and so on.) Too many prepositional phrases (even two in a row) can slow down the reader. Good writers avoid clustering together too many phrases.

Rewrite the five sentences in the "Activity" in the brown box on p. 448 of your textbook. Try to avoid using strings of prepositional phrases, but also try to keep all the information in the sentences. If required, submit your revisions to your instructor for evaluation.

ANSWER KEY

| | Learning | Focus | |
|Answer | Objectives | Points | References |

I. Writing Activity: Invention
..........LO 1..............FP 1..video segment 1; textbook, p. 432
(Your instructor will advise you about evaluating this assignment.)

II. Writing Activity: Opening and Closing Paragraphs
..........LO 5..............FP 14.......................... video segment 6; textbook, pp. 406–451, 752–753
(Your instructor will advise you about evaluating this assignment.)

III. Writing Activity: Voice (Preachiness and Projecting Wonder)
..........LO 4..........FP 11, 12, 13, 14...video segment 5;
.... textbook, pp. 416–420, 426–427, 446–447
(Your instructor will advise you about evaluating this assignment.)

IV. Writing Activity: Strings of Phrases
..........LO 5..............FP 14..video segment 6; textbook, pp. 448, 802
(Your instructor will advise you about evaluating this assignment.)

Lesson 11

Imagining Solutions

An undefined problem has an infinite number of solutions.
—Robert A. Humphrey

THEME

Throughout this course, you are encouraged to look beyond the obvious, to see below the surface, and to think critically about each topic you examine. In this lesson, "Imagining Solutions," you will continue to ponder and discover the solutions you propose to a problem. You will present your solutions in a deeper context to your readers. For example, in your everyday life, you examine issues and problems and sort out the answers. Obviously, engaging the mind in seeking out the best solutions is a high level task. Additionally, figuring out the answers logically also allows you to think at optimum levels. For this assignment, you will involve yourself in analysis of a particular problem, development of criteria relevant to the possible solutions, and ways to determine the most favorable solution based on your research and your own measured and objective thought.

Once you have discovered a problem or topic that "lurks behind the obvious," you will delve beneath its layers. You will address the causes of the problem and try to decide what effect the solutions you imagine might have. You will imagine alternative solutions and construct support for each of them by examining logical fallacies. You will test strategies for presenting the problem, alternatives, criteria, and possible solutions in your writing. Try to accomplish growth beyond your original thinking by aiming for a higher level of analysis.

It's so much easier to suggest solutions when you don't know too much about the problem.
—Malcolm Forbes

LESSON RESOURCES

Textbook: Mauk and Metz: *The Composition of Everyday Life*
- Chapter 10, "Proposing Solutions," pp. 452–501
- Chapter 6, "Logical Fallacies," p. 290
- Chapter 15, "Rhetorical Handbook"
    - "Agreement," pp. 768–771
    - "Verb," pp. 792–799

Video: "Imagining Solutions" from the series *The Writer's Circle*

LESSON GOAL

You will communicate to readers a written argument that a problem must be addressed, that action is necessary, and that the proposed solution has value.

LESSON LEARNING OBJECTIVES

1. Discover a problem that needs rethinking.
2. Analyze the causes of the problem that needs rethinking.
3. Include the key elements of argument (organization, thesis, support, counterargument, concessions) in proposing the solution to a problem.
4. Hone analytical and sentence skills in revising an argument that solves a particular problem.

LESSON FOCUS POINTS

1. How does a writer find a topic for a problem-solving argument?
2. What are ways a writer can analyze the problem?
3. What are ways a writer can find solutions?
4. What are the key elements in articulating a thesis for a solution argument?
5. What is counterargument and how might a writer use this tool in an argumentative paper of solution? How does a writer find appropriate counterarguments? Where should a writer include counterarguments?
6. What are alternative solutions and how will a writer find ways to articulate those alternatives? How does a writer find the shortcomings and strengths of alternative solutions?
7. What are concessions/qualifiers? How will they assist a writer in arguing a solution?
8. What are the ways a writer may construct supporting points for an argument of solution? What are techniques a writer may use to invite the reader to be involved in the argument of solution?
9. What are logical fallacies associated with sorting out solutions in an argument? How might a writer avoid logical fallacies?
10. What are turnabout paragraphs? How can they assist a writer of problem and solution?
11. What is reasonable tone? How may a writer create reasonable tone in an argument of problem and solution?
12. Why is verb mood an important element of an argument of problem and solution?
13. Why is revision important in an argumentative paper of problem and solution?

WRITERS INTERVIEWED

Gretchen Sween, Attorney and Writer, Dallas TX
Macarena Hernandez, Editorial Columnist, *The Dallas Morning News,* Dallas TX

SUGGESTED WRITING ASSIGNMENTS

Consult with your instructor and the course syllabus about requirements for any of the assignments listed below.

1. Write an essay addressing a problem, suggesting actions to address the problem, and convincing the reader that the proposed solution is valuable.
2. Write a letter addressing your problem and proposing a solution to someone who can take action on it.
3. Find an image that relates to your essay. Write a caption for it, and then write an essay explaining the relationship between the image and your text.

As long as anyone believes that his ideal and purpose is outside him, that it is above the clouds, in the past or in the future, he will go outside himself and seek fulfillment where it cannot be found. He will look for solutions and answers at every point except where they can be found--in himself.
—Erich Frohm

ENRICHMENT ACTIVITIES

Complete the following activities. An answer key and/or guidelines appear at the end of this lesson for each activity.

I. Writing Activity: Organizational Strategies in Richard's Essay
Read the following selections from a draft of Richard's essay. Outline the essay and identify the problem and proposed solutions. What organizational strategy did Richard use to arrange his argument? In your opinion, is it the best arrangement or should he have opted for another arrangement? (See p. 494 in your text.) What suggestions do you have for supporting the solution(s) Richard is forwarding to his audience?

Like many white Americans, I have a dirty secret. My ancestors owned slaves. This is not exactly the kind of thing people expect to find when they go searching through their genealogy looking for colorful characters and heroic deeds to which they can claim a historical connection.

When I came across this distasteful fact, my first reaction was denial. The second was a kind of internal shrug: Oh well, I thought, that was a long time ago and it doesn't have anything to do with me. I've never owned slaves, or defended slavery or profited from slavery. My only connection to it is an accident of birth. That is true

Lesson 11—Imagining Solutions

enough as far as it goes. But the problem with this line of thinking is that it doesn't go far enough. The problem is that it is assumes that the legacy of slavery affects only black people. After all, white people were the perpetrators not the victims in the crime of slavery. So if you're white, no problem, right? Wrong.

The legacy of slavery is racism, segregation, and racial inequality. Blacks experience the insult, and the many disadvantages of this legacy. What do whites experience? Racial privilege. Wait a minute, you're thinking, I don't experience that. I don't even know what that is. If that's what you're thinking, you've just proved my point. We aren't aware of racial privilege because we've been taught not to pay attention to it. Our legacy is our own obliviousness.

People who are spoiled are typically unaware of the fact that they're spoiled, or of the effect that their sense of entitlement has on others. A spoiled individual has an unrealistic and self-centered view of the world. Their inflated expectations make them insensitive to the needs of others. When a person is spoiled, we consider that person to have a problem. And the problem they have makes them a problem for others.

The problem may be hard to see at first, but the solution is obvious. Because the minute you begin to pay attention to it, it begins to recede. When we become conscious of the privileges we receive because of our race, we automatically become more conscious of the disadvantages people of other races experience. Most of us do not expect special privileges in life. We don't like the thought of benefiting at someone else's expense. It makes us uncomfortable. And in a sense, isn't that all it would take to undermine the legacy of slavery? If all of the white people in America suddenly felt uncomfortable with white privilege and racial discrimination, something would have to change.

Whether your ancestors were slaves or slave owners, free blacks or poor whites, or immigrants who came to this country after the Civil War, you are living in a society shaped by the legacy of slavery. And that legacy affects all of us. If you're black, it means you've probably experienced some of the humiliations and hardships of racism. If you're white, it means you've had advantages and opportunities you're probably not even aware of. Now doesn't that make you just a little bit uncomfortable?

If required, submit your outline and your suggestions for organization to your instructor for grading.

II. Writing Activity: Organizational Strategies for Finding Solutions
Read the essay by Paul Roberts, "How to Say Nothing in 500 Words" on pp. 464-469 in your textbook. Analyze Roberts' organizational strategies in a brief essay for your instructor. What is the problem and how does Roberts clarify it for the reader? What specific examples really stand out for you as a reader? How does Roberts employ "lively language"? List several examples of lively language from your reading of the essay.

If required, submit your response to your instructor for evaluation.

III. Writing Activity: Logical Fallacies
Read pp. 289–290 and p. 493 in your textbook. Review the examples of logical fallacies below to determine their identity. For each fallacy, choose the appropriate response from the following list. Use the answer key to check your choices. Write a brief essay explaining why each example fits its identifier. If required, submit the essay to your instructor for evaluation.

Logical fallacies:

A. Begging the question
B. Ad hominem
C. False analogy
D. Faulty cause and effect

E. Hasty generalization
F. Slippery slope
G. Straw person

_____ 1. You shouldn't give people extra privileges. If you do, they'll take advantage of you all the time.

_____ 2. Sue: I believe that war is morally wrong.
Joe: Of course you will say that, you are a pacifist.
Sue: How about the arguments I just gave you in support of my position on war?
Joe: Those don't matter. Like I said, you are a pacifist, so you have to say that war is morally wrong. Also, you lead peace marches, so I can't believe what you say.

_____ 3. Senator Smith-Jones says that we should not fund the attack submarine program. It is so difficult for me to understand why he is encouraging the Senate to leave us defenseless like that.

_____ 4. If Polly's actions were not illegal, then they would not be prohibited by law.

_____ 5. Billy, you are going to have to make up your mind. Either you decide you can afford this iPod or decide you are going to do without music for a while.

_____ 6. Gloria is riding her bike in her home town in Indiana, minding her own business. A pickup truck comes up behind her. The driver starts honking his horn and then tries to force her off the road. As he goes by, the driver yells "Get on the bike path where you belong!" Gloria sees that the pickup has California plates and concludes that all California drivers are jerks.

_____ 7. Some people claim that severe illness is caused by depression and anger. After all, people who are severely ill are depressed and angry. Thus, it follows that the cause of severe illness actually is the depression and anger. So, a good and cheerful attitude is key to staying healthy.

If required, submit a paper explaining the relationship between each example and logical fallacy to your instructor for evaluation.

ANSWER KEY

Answer	Learning Objectives	Focus Points	References

I. Writing Activity: Organizational Strategies in Richard's Essay
............LO 2, 3..........FP 1–7, 9, 14................................video segments 3, 4; textbook, pp. 494–495
(Your instructor will advise you about evaluating this assignment.)

II. Writing Activity: Organizational Strategies for Finding Solutions
............LO 2, 3..........FP 1–9, 12, 14..............................video segments 3, 4; textbook, pp. 494–495
(Your instructor will advise you about evaluating this assignment.)

III. Writing Activity: Logical Fallacies
(Several possibilities exist for the identification of logical fallacies. What follows are possible responses.)
1. F ....LO 4 ....FP 10 ....textbook, pp. 289–291, 493
2. B.........LO 4 ....FP 10 ....textbook, pp. 289–291, 493
3. G.........LO 4 ....FP 10 ....textbook, pp. 289–291, 493
4. A.........LO 4 ....FP 10 ....textbook, pp. 289–291, 493
5. C.........LO 4 ....FP 10 ....textbook, pp. 289–291, 493
6. E ....LO 4 ....FP 10 ....textbook, pp. 289–291, 493
7. D.........LO 4 ....FP 10 ....textbook, pp. 289–291, 493

Lesson 12

Discovering Voice

I am enough of an artist to draw freely upon my imagination. Imagination is more important than knowledge. Knowledge is limited. Imagination encircles the world.

—Albert Einstein

THEME

Art, in whatever form, offers something to our everyday experience. Perhaps art offers answers to the gnawing uncertainties of daily existence, or mystery and intensity in a world that seems too plain. Art offers a framework for exploring people's behavior or even a deeper understanding of our place in society. Exploring and responding to the arts is the process of developing and communicating ideas, not simply about a painting, a sonata, a sculpture, or a drama, but about life.

Becoming familiar with the concept of the artist's voice is one aspect of exploring the arts, since voice reflects the writer's personal style of expression. Appropriate word choice, rhythm, repetition, sentence structure, and the tempo of your language all contribute to voice in writing. All writers have distinctive voices, an inherent quality of the individual writer's style, talent, and vision.

In this lesson, you will discover your voice by exploring a work of art whether it be a painting, a sonata, a sculpture, or a drama to find the connection between that object and the world at large. Let the art invite you into its realm. Become that piece of art, that skyscraper, landscape, poem, or song. Live it. Breathe it. Understand its every nuance. Explore its exterior and interior. Love its faults. Adore its strengths. Then, determine what you might write about it. Communicate to your audience that which you have come to know better than yourself. Let your imagination soar to its highest. Release your inner voice.

The object of art is not to reproduce reality, but to create a reality of the same intensity.

—Alberto Giacometti

LESSON RESOURCES

Textbook: Mauk and Metz: *The Composition of Everyday Life*
- Chapter 11, "Exploring the Arts," pp. 502–559
- Chapter 15, "Rhetorical Handbook"
  - "Writing Style," pp.754–756
  - "Word Choice," pp.775–777

Video: "Discovering Voice" from the series *The Writer's Circle*

LESSON GOAL

You will communicate that art is an investigation into human thought and imagination as well as culture and society.

LESSON LEARNING OBJECTIVES

1. Analyze a work of art through reading and discussion.
2. Develop a specific point about the work of art that explains why or how the work makes a difference in everyday life.
3. Communicate ideas about the work or works of art to an audience using the elements of evaluation.
4. Explore ways to refine the key elements of the argument.
5. Refine the writer's voice to promote wonder and to avoid over-enthusiasm and harsh description in an argument about a work of art.

LESSON FOCUS POINTS

1. Why should a writer discover the genres of literature and their relationship to a literary work? What points should a writer examine about a musical work? What are the various mediums of visual arts?
2. Why do titles of works of art matter? Why are they relevant to an argument?
3. Why are form and composition and color important to discuss in an argument about visual art?
4. What does a writer need to know about film in order to analyze and evaluate a particular film? Why are the title, plot, characters, and setting important to an analysis of a film?
5. What is theme in a work of art? Why should a writer address it? What is conflict in a work of art? Why should a writer address conflict?

6. What is character development in a work of art? Why should a writer address character?
7. What are the conventions surrounding a particular work of art? Why is it necessary for a writer to be familiar with conventions?
8. Why is style critical to the examination of a work of art for evaluative purposes?
9. What is context? How does it relate to an argument of analysis of a work of art?
10. Why should others care about the analysis of a particular work of art? How can a writer assist the audience in understanding the underlying meanings of a work of art?
11. Why is thesis important in the analysis of a work of art?
12. How does a writer develop support for an analysis of a work of art? What are the elements of evaluation? How can those elements assist a writer in examining a work of art?
13. What is the best way to present the information in an analysis/evaluation of a work of art? How can a writer integrate lines from the work of art into the body of an evaluation?
14. How does a writer avoid the enthusiasm crisis? How does a writer avoid harsh description? How does a writer promote wonder?

WRITERS INTERVIEWED

Laeta Kalogridis, Screenwriter, Encino CA
Naomi Shihab Nye, Author and Poet, San Antonio TX
Matt Zoller Seitz, Film and Television Critic, *New York Press/Newark Star-Ledger,* Brooklyn NY

SUGGESTED WRITING ASSIGNMENTS

Consult with your instructor and the course syllabus about requirements for any of the assignments listed below.

1. Write an essay of analysis in which you research and discuss a work or works of art in an argument.
2. Consider two of the following works of art: The Empire State Building, the movie *Titanic,* Aretha Franklin's song "Respect," Leonardo da Vinci's *The Last Supper,* Woodie Guthrie's song "This Land is Your Land," the Taj Majal. In an essay, discuss how each of those two works may have been influenced by its context (political, cultural, aesthetic climate).
3. Write a "found poem" based on the essay you wrote in assignment #1 above. (See pp. 558–559 in your textbook.

It would be a mistake to ascribe this creative power to an inborn talent. In art, the genius creator is not just a gifted being, but a person who has succeeded in arranging for their appointed end, a complex of activities, of which the work is the outcome. The artist begins with a vision—a creative operation requiring an effort. Creativity takes courage.

—Henri Matisse

ENRICHMENT ACTIVITIES

Complete the following activities. An answer key or guidelines appear at the end of this lesson for each activity.

I. Writing Activity: Invention
Read the short story, "A Very Old Man with Enormous Wings" by Gabriel Garcia-Marquez in your textbook (pp. 507-510). In a brief essay, describe how you would analyze the short story. Be sure to discuss how you would address the plot, character, setting, narrator, and characters. How would you include a discussion of themes, conflict, conventions, and style? What about the context of the work?

If required, submit your essay to your instructor for grading.

II. Writing Activity: Thesis Problems
Examine your essay of analysis for thesis problems. Write a short essay explaining the thesis problems you encountered in writing your essay. To get you started, provide an example of each of the following thesis problems. (Please do not use the examples from your textbook):

1. **The obvious fact problem**: The obvious fact statement merely states what many people already know.

   Example: _____
   _____
   _____

2. **The personal opinion problem**: The most obvious form includes phrases such as "I think," "I love," or "I believe."

   Example: _____
   _____
   _____

3. **The overstated claim problem:** Writers must be cautious about projecting their inclinations too far and saying something that cannot be proven.

   Example: _____
   _____
   _____
   _____

4. **The summary problem:** Summary should only be a part of your analysis of a work of art and should work only to support a more analytical point.

   Example: _____
   _____
   _____
   _____
   _____
   _____

   If required, submit your short essay and the answers to the thesis problems to your instructor

III. **Writing Activity: Using the Elements of Evaluation**
   Read and review Marcus' essay for this lesson. Write a short essay of response to the following questions about his essay:

1. What does Marcus' subject of his essay try to achieve?
2. What do other similar subjects try to achieve?
3. Who is the audience for the subject?
4. What goals should this subject or all subjects like it have?
5. Through what particular ways does the subject achieve the goal? What specific parts, tools or strategies help the subject to achieve its goal?
6. In what particular ways does the subject fall short of achieving its goal?
7. What is unique about the subject's approach or strategy?

If required, submit your responses to your instructor for evaluation.

Marcus' Essay

Where would you go to see some of the world's greatest works of sculpture? Paris? Rome? London? Madrid? Consider the Nasher Sculpture Center, a venue that has made Dallas, Texas, an unlikely mecca for admirers of modern sculpture. The center showcases the premier private collection of modern sculpture in the world, a collection that was coveted by many museums before collector Raymond Nasher decided to build his own museum in the city where he resides. The majority of the space is devoted to an outdoor sculpture garden designed by landscape architect Peter Walker. His ingenious architectural design makes the sculpture seem right at home at the intersection of a highway and a busy downtown street, but what really transforms the Nasher Sculpture Center from an ordinary museum into an aesthetic triumph is not just the sculpture within its walls, but also the way the garden transforms the urban landscape beyond its walls.

In keeping with the intention of its benefactor to build a "roof-less" museum the garden of the Nasher Sculpture Center is enclosed by low walls, perhaps ten feet in height, that block out most of the city noise and the sight of traffic. Space within the garden is defined by trees, fountains, and bushes that seem to create viewing areas or open air "rooms" that separate and showcase the different sculptures. By definition, sculpture generally lacks the physical frame a painting has. Instead, it is framed by the environment and the objects around it. Placing the sculpture in a garden surrounded by trees, flowers, and fountains gives it a peaceful, contemplative context. Without having seen the garden, you might imagine a kind of cloistered feel, where the city is shut out and you are transported into an oasis of art and nature far from the world of commerce outside its walls.

But this garden doesn't shut the city out. Instead it includes the city, framing the skyscrapers that loom over it in a way that makes them look like larger sculptures. In this odd trick of proportion, a sculpture like Eviva Amore, a gigantic steel abstract structure that juts up into the sky, seems to bear a direct relationship to the skyscrapers beyond it. Walking to the Sky, a line of sculpted people walking up a pole into the clouds, seems to follow the vertical lines of the buildings around it, as if the people headed in the same direction as the skyscrapers. Following Peter Walker's architectural design, the walls of the garden contain large windows cut out in several places that also serve as frames, composing a tableau of a car passing on the street, a pedestrian walking on the sidewalk. They reinforce the aesthetic context, transforming the urban surroundings from ordinary downtown cityscape to a kind of found art.

The most dramatic sculpture at the Nasher is not really a sculpture at all, but a kind of architectural installation designed specifically for it called Tending (Blue). This piece is a trapezoid-shaped room with benches around the inside walls and a large opening in the ceiling that frames a square of the sky. It has the feel of a chapel or a kiva, a Native American sacred chamber with a hole at the top. Sitting in the room, you look up at the sky and simply stare, experiencing the empty space that is framed there. When a plane or a bird passes over, it floats in the frame for a moment, then passes out, leaving you with the feeling that an aesthetic event has just occurred and then come to an end, just as Peter Walker intended.

The effect of Walker's landscape design at the Nasher may be most noticeable when you leave. As you walk back out onto the street from the garden, there in front of you are the buildings that seemed so much more intimate and (how else can I put it?) sculptural, only a moment before. The illusion is gone, making you long to return to the garden where the skyscrapers reveal themselves to be art.

IV. **Writing Activity: Writer's Voice**
Review Marcus's essay printed in Writing Activity III to check his voice. Is he over-enthusiastic? Is he harsh in his description? Does he promote wonder? Does he consider the tone of the art? Each item is described below.

Avoiding the Enthusiasm Crisis: to avoid enthusiasm, pay attention to the following:
- Overly positive adjectives.
- Unsupported judgments.
- Overly broad claims about the art or artist.

Avoiding Harsh Description
- Draws attention to the emotions of the speaker rather than inviting reflection.
- Language overshadows any particular elements of the subject.
- Language draws attention to itself.
- Best to steer toward subtlety.

Promoting Wonder
- Writing about art should create intensity and make the writer and reader feel a sense of wonder.
- Wonder shows the reader powerful aspects of the artistic work.
- A writer can embody the kind of wonder he wants to bestow on readers.
- Writers use language and sentence structure that dramatize the thoughts and feelings associated with the work.

Considering the Tone of the Art
- A writer's voice depends on the subject.
- Writers shouldn't fall entirely in line with their subjects.
- Writers pay attention to the formality of voice in describing their subjects.
- Some writers present distinct voices that are different from the art they discuss.

Write an essay to submit to your instructor about Marcus' voice in his essay. Quote specific passages from the essay that present his voice to you. When is he overly enthusiastic about the sculpture garden? Are his descriptions harsh and overly emotional? Does he promote wonder? Does he consider the tone of the art in his presentation? If required, submit your essay to your instructor for evaluation.

ANSWER KEY

Answer	Learning Objectives	Focus Points	References

I. Writing Activity: Invention
................LO 1, 2 ....FP 1–3, 5, 6 ....video segment 7; textbook, pp. 537–543
(Your instructor will advise you about evaluating this assignment.)

II. Writing Activity: Thesis Problem
................LO 2, 3 ....FP 11 ....video segment 2; textbook, pp. 546–547
(Your instructor will advise you about evaluating this assignment.)

III. Writing Activity: Using the Elements of Evaluation
................LO 3, 4 ....FP 12, 13 .... video segments 4, 7; textbook, pp. 550–551
(Your instructor will advise you about evaluating this assignment.)

IV. Writing Activity: Writer's Voice
.................LO 5 ....FP 14 .... video segments 1, 3, 4; textbook, pp. 554–556
(Your instructor will advise you about evaluating this assignment.)

Lesson 13

Thinking Radically

When you are right, you cannot be too radical; when you are wrong, you cannot be too conservative.
—Martin Luther King, Jr.

THEME

Radical thinking results in experimentation beyond the norms set by society. Radical thinking results in the invention of ideas beyond our wildest thinking. To think radically, you must transcend the conventional, even reform conventional thinking.

Throughout this course, you have learned and applied ways to communicate about yourself and your world by observation, analysis, argument, evaluation, exploration, and research. Try to think radically as you stir together all of the skills you have learned in this course to examine your topic. Try new approaches as the students in the coffee shop do in their collaborative writing. Try new ways of thinking as you explore a topic inside out and upside down. Try to examine all the dimensions of your topic to come up with a compelling, radical, different, and extreme argument for your final assignment in the course.

Any sufficiently advanced technology is indistinguishable from magic.
—Arthur C. Clarke

LESSON RESOURCES

Textbook: Mauk and Metz: *The Composition of Everyday Life*
- Chapter 12, "Thinking Radically: Re-seeing the World," pp. 560–609
- Chapter 15, "Rhetorical Handbook"
  – "Beyond the Five-Paragraph Essay," p. 749
  – "Coherence and Conciseness," pp. 761–764

Video: "Thinking Radically" from the series *The Writer's Circle*

LESSON GOAL

You will escape conventional thinking to imagine and write an argument about something outside common intellectual activity.

LESSON LEARNING OBJECTIVES

1. Discover a new idea by questioning, imagining, and exploring unconventional possibilities.
2. Develop a focused thesis using rhetorical tools to develop thoughts.
3. Apply the support strategies of evidence and appeals in developing an argument using radical thinking.
4. Engage readers by paying particular attention to tone and voice in an argument of radical thought.
5. Use global revision questions (arrangement, structure) to revise an argument of radical thought.

LESSON FOCUS POINTS

1. How does a writer imagine new connections, particularly in relationships? How does a writer imagine different possibilities in discovering a new idea? How does a writer question common sense?
2. In exploring the past and future, how does a writer discover a radical vision? How does a writer get to the "root" of radical thinking? How does exploration of a theory assist a writer in discovering radical thought?
3. How does a writer overturn conventional wisdom? How does a writer overcome writing clichés?
4. What questions assist a writer in getting away from conventional thinking? What are the best ways for a writer to connect to others when arguing radical thought?
5. How are outside sources helpful to a writer who is writing a radical argument?
6. How does a writer communicate a new vision on the topic? How does the thesis communicate the radical thought?
7. How is narration helpful to a writer when writing an argument of radical thought? How can description help a writer when writing an argument of radical thought? What can definitions do to further an argument of radical thought?
8. How can evidence (statistics, authorities, facts, examples, allusion, testimonies, anecdotes, scenarios) support an argument of radical thought?
9. How does figurative language assist in an argument of radical thought? How can appeals (logic, emotion, character, need, value) assist a writer in communicating an argument of radical thought?
10. What role does counterargument play in an argument of radical thought? How can concessions assist the argument of radical thought? How does Toulminian Analysis aid a writer of an argument of radical thought?

11. How should a writer begin an argument of radical thought? How are anecdotes, scenarios, allusions, figurative language, and questions helpful to a writer of an argument of radical thought?
12. In an argument of radical thought, how does a writer make connections to conventional thinking? How should an argument of radical thought conclude?
13. How does a writer avoid alienating the reader in an argument of radical thought? How does a writer project wonder in an argument of radical thought?
14. Why is revision particularly important in an argument of radical thought?
15. Who besides the instructor will benefit from the ideas in an argument of radical thought?

WRITERS INTERVIEWED

Eric Jerome Dickey, Novelist, Los Angeles, CA
Richard Rodriguez, Essayist and Journalist, San Francisco, CA
Matt Zoller Seitz, Film and Television Critic, *New York Press/Newark Star-Ledger,* Brooklyn, NY

SUGGESTED WRITING ASSIGNMENTS

Consult with your instructor and the course syllabus about requirements for any of the assignments listed below.

1. Write an argumentative essay of radical thought by communicating ideas about a particular subject outside common intellectual activity.
2. Select a topic from the "Point of Contact" section of your textbook on page 588. Then develop a thesis and write a rough draft of an essay based on one of the prompts.

> *If you follow your bliss, you put yourself on a kind of track that has been there all the while, waiting for you, and the life that you ought to be living is the one you are living. Wherever you are, if you are following your bliss, you are enjoying that refreshment, that life within you, all the time.*
> —Joseph Campbell

ENRICHMENT ACTIVITIES

Complete the following activities. An answer key and/or guidelines appear at the end of this lesson for each activity.

I. Writing Activity: Thesis

Choose five of the statements on p. 596 in your textbook. Describe how each statement is radical. Does it transcend or speak back to some particular conventional way of thinking? How does it reveal something usually overlooked or dismissed? How does the wording and construction of each sentence help the reader to see something new? Write at least one paragraph for each statement. Submit your work to your instructor for evaluation.

II. Writing Activity: Organizational Strategies

Read the essay by Doris Lessing, "Group Minds," on pages 583–584 in your textbook. Write an analysis of the organizational strategies Lessing employed to present her ideas.

1. How did she begin? Did she use an anecdote, a scenario, an allusion, figurative language or a question? Did that method work well?

2. How did she make connections to conventional thinking? Did she distinguish between conventional and radical thinking in separate paragraphs? Or did she use a turnabout paragraph to make a shift from conventional to radical thinking? How did her approach work for you, the reader?

3. How did Lessing conclude her essay? Did she make her connections and her claims relevant and valuable to the world shared by the writer and reader? Did Lessing use the most dramatic or direct means for connecting the idea to the reader in her conclusion? Was Lessing successful in her conclusion?

III. Writing Activity: The Writer's Style

Review the essay written in collaboration by the distance learning students in the lesson video. Then look at the checklist p. 608, "Peer Review" in your textbook. Using the checklist, evaluate the main style characteristics of each writer. Evaluate the separate voices and the overall voice of the piece itself. Devote at least a paragraph to each writer and the essay itself. If required, submit your response in writing to your instructor for evaluation.

SSEWBA (someday soon everything will be acronyms)

TEOTWAWKI (the end of the world as we know it)
by Marcus

The traditional elements of the essay—language, style, information and opinion -- have evolved over hundreds of years, but the basic structure has remained the same. A writer presents ideas in an independently conceived work that follows a generally accepted pattern of introduction, thesis, supporting arguments or evidence, and conclusion. It's worked for centuries—and it still works—but for how much longer? As Bob Dylan sang, "The times they are a-changin'." The structure of written communication, of literary expression, of journalism, and academic writing, is undergoing a radical transformation. As people all over the world discover the power of instant messaging, blogging, self-publishing and professional publishing on the Internet, they are engaging in a new global conversation. New forms of writing emerging on the Internet have unique literary and intellectual value, and should be seen as groundbreaking developments in the history of writing.

    The traditional monologue of the writer is giving way to a worldwide dialogue. It's a revolution that's spreading by word of mouse, and it's changing the way we read and write. The question is, "Is it changing for the better or for the worse?" If some argue that literary standards are being lowered by this unorthodox discourse, the volume of writing on the Internet is simply too large for anyone to actually judge its overall quality. But if quality is measured by the best of what's out there, instead of by the worst, then online writing may be the best thing to happen to writing since the Chinese invented paper.

GMTFT (Great minds think for themselves.)
by Jada

If the invention of paper made it possible for people to stop scratching their words onto stone tablets, then the Internet has made it possible for people to stop using paper. And paper is so 20th century. But it's not just what we write on and about that's changing; it's the structure of writing itself. The Internet is an instant, interactive mode of communication. It is constantly shifting and reacting, moving forward, circling back; it's not static: it's alive.

    In this brave new world of Internet writing, blogging may be the most radical act of all. Blogging is a form of writing that is part diary, part essay, part editorial, part conversation. Combining text with links, photos, graphics, excerpts from other blogs or online sources, audio and video clips, and even ads, blogs also incorporate comments from readers, replies to other bloggers, and references to previous posts or comment threads. Multimedia, intertextuality, and personal expression all combine into one radical new form of writing.

    Traditional publishing limits the number of published writers to authors who can negotiate contracts or afford the cost of self-publishing. The Internet has opened up a new medium for writers, and many are jumping in. It could be argued that this democratization of writing is lowering the standards of literature, but the opposite could also be true. After all, how many gifted writers throughout history were overlooked or never even discovered because the obstacles to publishing were too great?

But blogging isn't just for amateurs. Professional writers, columnists, even newspaper editorial boards now have blogs. Malcolm Gladwell blogs, Michael Moore blogs, Dave Barry blogs. Actors, athletes, artists, activists, politicians, pundits, and people who have no claim to fame at all blog. People like me. I would never have tried to write a column or an article or a book. But I have something to say, and blogging gives me a way to say it. The beauty of it is, many creative, fascinating, original people are blogging.

MWBRL (More will be revealed later.)

by Lakshmi

Blogs aren't the only new form of writing that has developed on the Internet. In the innovative universe of the Internet, few have discovered hypertext.

Hypertext is a non-linear narrative that a reader can enter from many different places and travel in many different directions. The reader decides how to read the text, when and whether to digress and which character to follow.

Hypertext may be written by several writers with simultaneous, overlapping, or interconnecting storylines. Even fiction and non-fiction are not clearly demarcated in hypertext, as writers may incorporate real events or experiences, even themselves as characters, in works that clearly have little interest in the distinction between fact and fiction. In one famous hypertext, *The Unknown,* the authors introduce themselves as characters, frequently commenting on their writing process and other real-life events as the story unfolds. Links in the text lead to biographies of the writers, or letters, or press coverage of their experimental writing.

Like previous groundbreaking forms of writing, (e.g., the modernist work of James Joyce), hypertext attempts to mimic stream of consciousness rather than impose a linear progression on its narrative. Diversity, digression, and self-awareness are the hallmarks of post-modern literature and of hypertext. Hypertext is avant-garde, even for online writing. Yet it may be the future of fiction. As readers seek out more content on the Internet rather than in bookstores, and as the level of exposure to alternative forms increases, hypertext is a natural progression to the next stage.

CMIIW (Correct me if I'm wrong.)
by Rosa

Although some may not understand what hypertext is, online writing has opened up whole new fields of publishing and information delivery. Online journalism has made up-to-the-minute information instantly available and accessible. Some of the biggest stories have been broken not by traditional news sources, but by bloggers or alternative websites. These alternative sources can publish information more rapidly than traditional news sources, partly because there's less bureaucracy, and partly because of less stringent fact-checking requirement. Anyone can publish on the Internet by creating a blog, writing a comment, sending an e-mail, or breaking a story. This makes it difficult for the truth to be suppressed. But the opportunities for error and deceit are just as great as the opportunities for truth.

While some are concerned with the dangers of misinformation or bad information, proponents of alternative online journalism argue that the Internet is a self-correcting system. They claim that bad information is exposed and good information surfaces.

Wikipedia, an online "open-source" encyclopedia is an example of a self-correcting system. According to its website, "Wikipedia is an encyclopedia written collaboratively by many of its readers." Contributors are constantly improving Wikipedia, making thousands of changes an hour, all of which are recorded. Wikipedia is doing more than producing a free online encyclopedia; it's turning its readers into writers and editors. It's a bottom-up sharing of knowledge, rather than a top-down dispensing of knowledge. This process makes Internet journalism more accessible, more diverse, more democratic, and less formal. It's more than just a new form of journalism; it's a new intellectual paradigm.

TWIWI? (That was interesting, wasn't it?)
by Richard

Radical transformations, worldwide conversations, revolutionary new forms of writing, new intellectual paradigms...these are adventurous claims. Is there really anything new here? And, if there is, is it really worthy of the name literature, or even journalism? There's something happening to writing, that much is indisputable. Look at people emailing and text messaging, using abbreviations and acronyms, communicating in a pseudo-language that reduces complex thoughts and emotions to semi-intelligible symbols. At least, that's one way of looking at it. But there's another. The verbal economy of instant messaging has spawned a whole new realm of creativity. Not only new forms of writing, but a new language is being invented by a new nation of speakers.

    This blurring of the lines between speaking and writing is at the heart of the change that's being wrought by online writing. What the Internet has made possible is a worldwide written conversation, that's influencing all writers, amateurs and professionals alike. The literary and the intellectual value of these new forms of writing emerges from the surprising genius of ordinary people, few of whom are ever actually ordinary.

RUUP4IT?

ANSWER KEY

Answer	Learning Objectives	Focus Points	References

I. Writing Activity: Thesis
................LO 1, 2.................FP 6...video segment 1; textbook, pp. 596–597
(Your instructor will advise you about evaluating this assignment.)

II. Writing Activity: Organizational Strategies
................LO 3................FP 11–12................................... video segments 3, 4; textbook, pp. 602–603
(Your instructor will advise you about evaluating this assignment.)

III. Writing Activity: The Writer's Voice
................LO 4, 5.............FP 13–14................................video segment 6; textbook, pp. 604–605, 608
(Your instructor will advise you about evaluating this assignment.)